If Clouds Could Talk

Read & enjoy !
Garth

by Garth Wallace

Published by
Happy Landings

Other books by Garth Wallace:

Fly Yellow Side Up
Pie In The Sky
Derry Air
Cockpit Follies
The Flying Circus
Don't Call Me a Legend
Blue Collar Pilots

National Library of Canada Cataloguing in Publication

If Clouds Could Talk
fiction, aviation, humour

Written by: Garth Wallace

ISBN 0-9697322-9-5

    I. Title.

PS8595.A56516I5 2003   C813'.54   C2003-905242-7

Cover and inside artwork by: Francois Bougie

Editing: Liz Wallace, Sari Funston

Layout and typesetting: Happy Landings

Written, illustrated, typeset, printed and bound in Canada

Published by:

Happy Landings
RR #4
Merrickville, Ontario
K0G 1N0
Tel.: 613-269-2552
Fax: 613-269-3962
E-mail: books@happylandings.com
Web site: www.happylandings.com

If Clouds Could Talk

Contents

Introduction

When you think of business aviation, what comes to mind? How about a sleek corporate jet flown by two grey-haired pilots with a couple of high-level executives riding opulently in the back on their way to a large metropolis?

If that's your picture, it's about to change as you read this book.

Fasten your seat belts and crank up your sense of humour. If clouds could stop laughing and talk, this book is what they would say about corporate flying.

Garth Wallace

Dedication

This book is dedicated to members of the Mile High Club.

Chapter One

Pretzel Aviation

"**D**o you want any stunts tonight, Don?" I asked from the pilot's seat. Don Hitchcock was squeezing his portly frame into the back of his corporate airplane.

My passenger smiled. "Well, it's been a good week," he declared, plopping himself down in the seat. "How about a couple of victory rolls after takeoff?"

"Aye, aye, sir. Coming right up."

I started the engine. Don fastened his seat belts. I called the ground controller for taxi instructions.

"I've been telling people that my pilot works nights as a roller coaster operator," Don chuckled. "That's why he can't fly straight and level."

We were cleared to taxi to the runway.

"Seat belts tight, Don?" I called out.

He laughed. "With my girth they're tight when they're loose!"

Don Hitchcock was a politician. He looked the part. Thinning hair topped a round face. A cheesy smile connected his chubby cheeks. Sloping shoulders drooped all the way to his bourbon belly.

Don's idea of a corporate airplane was eccentric and practical at the same time. He was looking for something to shuttle him to and from work so he bought a Champion Citabria, a two-seat, fabric-covered, aerobatic airplane. When it wasn't flying Don, it earned money on a lease arrangement at the flying school that I operated with a partner.

We took off from the Toronto Island Airport and headed southwest along the Lake Ontario shoreline. Five miles later, the air traffic controller cleared us from his frequency. I acknowledged, eased the airplane's nose down slightly and let the speed build to 120 mph. Then I pulled the Citabria's nose up to the horizon, added power and pushed the control stick over. The wings rolled left and the shoreline rotated right.

As we passed through inverted, Don sang out, "With my pilot you can't throw up. You never know which way up is!"

The wings came around to level. I neutralized the controls.

Flying Don to work and back was my first corporate aviation job. On this trip, I had ferried the aircraft empty from the City of Circus, near Niagara Falls, to Toronto on a Friday afternoon to pick him up.

"My pilot flies for Pretzel Aviation," Don hooted. "When we're not upside down, we're inside out!"

I rolled the airplane to the right.

"Yahoo!" my irrepressible passenger cheered. "What does this look like on radar?"

"Pretzel sounds good," I replied. "Do you want to try one?"

"Naw, not tonight. I'd rather have a refreshment."

When we were level again, I reached under my seat and unzipped a pocket built in specially for Don. I pulled out a bottle of bourbon and a glass and held them over my shoulder.

"Don't mind if I do," Don said reaching for them. "A man's got to have some vice."

I could hear the liquid gurgling out of the bottle. The sweet smell of alcohol filled the small cockpit.

"Care to join me?" he asked.

"No thanks."

"You probably drank your way over," he giggled. "Well, here's a toast to the women you fly in my airplane."

"Sure, Don. You think I spend all week teaching aerobatics to beautiful girls."

"If clouds could talk, they'd tell me what you young pilots do up here," he declared. "I bet you slide on those aviator sunglasses, flash that sly smile and get all the women you want."

I didn't reply.

"I knew it," he chuckled. "You're probably the greatest womanizer in the City of Circus. I wish I were a few years younger and many pounds lighter," he said slapping his belly. "I'd buy sunglasses and pick up the broken-hearted women that you cast off."

"We sell sunglasses at the flying school," I said with a smile.

"Hee, hee. Now you're teasing an old man."

Chapter Two

Red seat covers

I had met Don Hitchcock after my flying school partner Henry Rains and I decided to expand our small operation. The idea started during one of our "business meetings" in the hangar.

"We're in a rut, Henry," I declared as I cleaned the windshield on one of our Piper Cherokees.

Henry was adding oil to the engine. "You call it a rut," he replied, "I'd call it a downdraft. We need to diversify."

Henry and I had started a flying school in the City of Circus. It was a shoestring operation but it was ours. We had leased two old Cherokee 140s from our former boss at another school. We borrowed money to build a hangar and buy a portable office. We believed that success would come through enthusiasm and hard work. "Make it fun and they will come," was our unofficial motto. We named the operation, "The Flying Circus."

Business had been brisk during the first six months. It was so good that we had hired staff. Henry's wife Leanne was enlisted as a receptionist, bookkeeper, dispatcher, janitor and nurse. Barry McDay, an air traffic controller in the Circus Tower, filled in as a part-time flying instructor. Barry's sister Summer, a student at the local university, traded reception duties for flying lessons. Chainsaw Charlie was a high school student who cleaned airplanes for us on the weekends.

But now winter was approaching. New students were harder to find. Our dream of being in business was in danger.

"Daytime Mondays to Fridays are the slowest," Henry offered. "How about selling business charters to increase our income?"

He pulled the empty plastic oil container from the engine access door and reached for another one.

I liked Henry. We had met while working for another operation as flying instructors. His head was screwed on right and most of the time he knew how to use it. This wasn't one of those times.

"Henry, no businessman is going to pay us to fly in these beat-up, little training airplanes."

Henry tipped up the other quart of oil. "You may be right, but the airplanes are here, they're insured and we're ready to go. It's worth a try."

I sprayed plastic cleaner on the other half of the bug-covered windshield. "Corporate aviation is about prestige, luxury, speed and dollar-be-damned," I said.

"Well then, we have a chance," he replied, holding the second can upside down. "The Cherokees might be slow compared to a Learjet but they beat driving. If business people equate prestige to money spent, then we'll overcharge. For luxury, I'll ask Leanne to make seat covers."

Henry had been raised on a western grain farm. Prestige was not part of his vocabulary, speed was not important and luxury was measured in the thickness of the red seat covers.

"You're an incurable optimist," I said, shaking my head.

I had to appreciate Henry's enthusiasm even though I knew the scheme wouldn't work. Besides, I couldn't talk him out of it.

Leanne stitched one set of red seat covers from a pair of old brocade curtains. We kept them under the counter in our tiny office ready to be installed in any airplane going on a charter flight.

Henry placed a small advertisement in the local newspaper.

No time to spare?
Go by air.
First class, on-demand,
Executive Charter Flights
Call The Flying Circus

Chapter Three

Look who's flying

We received our first call for a charter flight when I was working in the office alone.

"Good morning, The Flying Circus."

"Hi, this is Don Hitchcock. I saw your ad and I'd like to book a charter flight."

The request caught me off guard. "Ah, yes sir," I blurted out. "Ah, our airplanes are not large."

"Well, I may be fat," the man snorted, "but I think I can fit in a plane."

"I, ah, I mean we fly four-seaters," I said. "The maximum passenger load is three."

"The charter is for myself," he replied. He sounded cheerful.

"Ah, fine sir, but you should know that these are not long-range corporate aircraft." I realized that I was unselling our charter service but I didn't want to promise the man something that we couldn't deliver.

"Can they make it to Toronto?" he asked with a chuckle.

"Ah, yes sir, no problem," I said, recovering. "A short flight over to Toronto would be an easy trip in one of our Piper aircraft."

"Good. I'll book Monday morning departing at seven-thirty."

"Fine, sir," I replied. "Ah..."

"Click." He had hung up.

I sat there with the dead receiver in my hand. Unanswered questions flooded into my head. Did the man know where we were located? Did he want us to wait for him in Toronto or did he intend for us to return for him some other time? If the weather was bad, what was his phone number? Never mind his phone number, I couldn't remember the man's name.

As a feeling of stupidity sank in, Henry walked through the door. "Hi," he said with a smile. Then he saw the puzzled look on my face.

"You look a little stunned."

"Ah, yeah. I just took a request for our first charter."
His face lit up. "That's great! Who called?"
"I don't know," I replied.
"You don't know?"
"Right. I forgot his name."
"Well, don't worry about it. Just call him back and ask."
"I didn't get his phone number," I replied sheepishly.
"OK," Henry replied more slowly. "Tell me what you did get."
"Well, he wants to go to Toronto Island on Monday."
I wracked my brain for more information.
"This Monday or next Monday?" Henry asked patiently.
"Monday," I replied.
"OK. We have a charter flight some Monday for a mystery passenger.
"Are we waiting or dropping him off?"
"I don't know."
"Do we know how many people we are carrying for this man?"
"Yes. One."
"Good. And do we know when Mr. Mystery wants to depart?"

"Yes again," I said, triumphantly, "seven-thirty."

"A.m. or p.m.?"

My face dropped, then I remembered. "Morning."

"OK. You book one of the airplanes off for this Monday for three hours starting at seven-thirty. If he wants us to wait longer you can fly back here, do some lessons and pick him up later. I'll make up a charter question checklist for beside the telephone so we don't get stuck for answers on the next call."

I was lucky that Henry was so easy going. I booked the airplane for Monday morning. It felt good to think about flying somewhere different even if the destination was in sight of our home base on a clear day.

At 7:30 a.m. Monday I was standing beside our best looking Cherokee. It was parked on the ramp on a cool morning in October. I didn't know if the mystery passenger would show but I was thankful the weather was clear in case he did.

A few minutes later, a big boat of a Buick pulled into our parking lot. A large, older man got out. He retrieved an overcoat, a briefcase and an overnight bag from the Buick's back seat.

"Hi, there," his voice boomed from the parking lot. "Are you my pilot?"

"Yes, sir," I replied. I walked toward him and introduced myself. "Let me help you with your things."

The smiling passenger shifted his briefcase and coat to his left hand and offered me a rousing handshake. "I'm Don Hitchcock."

Don Hitchcock, Don Hitchcock. I burned the name into my brain. "Pleased to meet you, sir."

I took his overnight bag. It was then I realized that this customer might be the Member of Parliament Don Hitchcock. We walked toward the Cherokee.

"And this must be our substitute Learjet," Don said with a laugh.

"Yes sir," I answered. I must have had a worried look on my face.

"Oh, this will do just fine," he added quickly as we walked around the airplane's tail.

"I'll put the baggage on the back seat," I said reaching for the rest of his things, "then I'll slide into the left seat and you get in next."

"OK," he said, clapping and rubbing his hands together. "I'm ready to blast off when you are."

I climbed in. The man was heavy enough that the Cherokee sagged on the right side when he pulled himself onto the wingwalk beside the open door. He dropped into the right seat.

"Your male secretary warned me that the airplanes were small," he said with a grin.

I extended his lap harness fully before it would buckle together.

"This reminds me of my wife putting on a girdle," he giggled. "She doesn't bother anymore. Just let's it all hang out like I do."

I smiled, started the engine and called ground control for taxi instructions. I had already run the engine up and checked the systems. I switched to the tower controller while still moving toward the runway.

"Cherokee Lima Oscar Uniform Delta, ready for takeoff," I announced into the microphone. "Request right turn out for Toronto."

"Cleared for takeoff Oscar Uniform Delta, right turn approved, wind two two zero at five."

"Oscar Uniform Delta."

My passenger watched me work the controls for the takeoff. During the climbout, he said, "You make it look easy."

"It is easy," I replied.

"Oh, I don't know. You're talking to a man who rode a tricycle until he was 14," he said with a laugh.

I flew with one hand, reached behind us with the other and grabbed a thermos bottle from the back seat. The dented steel container had come from Henry's house.

"Would you like a coffee, sir?" I asked.

"Wow, coffee, tea or me," he chuckled.

"Just coffee," I replied. "I hope you like cream and sugar."

"OK, if you don't have anything stronger. I'll hold the cups. Can you pour, fly and breathe at the same time?"

"No problem." I poured two cups of the brown liquid.

We flew along the shore of Lake Ontario at 2,500 feet sipping coffee. It was a beautiful, calm, clear morning. I was enjoying the smooth ride and the scenery. It was a treat to be going somewhere without having to teach a student pilot how to get there.

My passenger told me that he lived near Circus but his office was in Toronto. "This is going to work out perfectly," he declared, looking down at the congestion of cars moving slowly on the highway. "I hate bucking that traffic."

He explained that he lived in an apartment in Toronto during the week.

"Are you the Member of Parliament Don Hitchcock?" I asked.

"One and the same," he replied heartily. "Have we met before?"

"No, but you look and sound important," I said.

"Aha! Buttering both sides of the bread, are we? Well son, you're trying to make a silk purse from a sow's ear, but I like it. You keep shoveling and you'd do well in politics, but wait until I retire."

"Yes, sir. It's a deal," I replied.

Don watched me fly. "Is this a training airplane?" he asked, pointing to the extra set of controls in front of him.

"Yes sir, it is."

"Don, call me Don. So could I learn to fly while commuting to and from work?"

I hesitated. "Ah... yes, I suppose you could."

His chubby face brightened.

"Go ahead," I offered. "Place your free hand lightly on the control wheel and your feet on the rudder pedals."

I didn't have to ask him twice. Don jammed his cup of coffee between his legs and then grabbed the control wheel with both hands. I stopped sightseeing and guided him through some basic manoeuvres on the way to Toronto. He was not a natural pilot but he was having fun. He attacked flying with boistrous enthusiasm. The result was an airplane zigzagging all over the sky. I had to continually correct him otherwise we would have never made it to Toronto.

"Hey, hey," Don exclaimed. "Look who's flying now!"

"You're doing very well, sir," I lied.

Before arriving at the Toronto Island Airport, I established that Don wanted me to return for him on Friday afternoon.

"Can I fly back?" he asked.

"Sure thing."

We landed and parked in front of the old wooden terminal building. Don climbed out. I passed him his coat, bag and briefcase from the back seat. He handed me a set of keys.

"They're for my car," he explained. "You might as well drive it while I'm here."

I started to protest but he waved me off. "See you Friday," he said. He turned and walked toward the nearby ferry dock. A boat ran every 15 minutes across the harbour to the downtown core.

On Friday I was at the Island Airport in good time. I met Don at the ferry dock. "Good afternoon, sir," I said reaching for his overnight bag.

"Thank you, but you have to cut the 'sir' stuff," he chuckled. "I get that all week. I'm beginning to believe I'm important. Call me Don."

"OK Don. We're parked right over here."

"That's better. Now tell me how many notches you carved in the dash of the Buick."

I had no idea what he was talking about. "Pardon me?"

"Scores. How many women did you score in my Buick?"

"None," I replied with a smile.

"I'm disappointed. It was making me feel good just to know that my car was getting lucky while I was working my butt off for the voters."

We loaded Don's bags into the Cherokee and climbed in. I explained a little about what I was doing while starting the airplane and taxiing out. We took off from Runway 28. A straight-out departure headed us westbound along the north shore of Lake Ontario. I leveled off at 1,500 feet.

"You have control," I said.

We sashayed along the shoreline under Don's unsteady hand. I talked him through some manoeuvres on the Private Pilot Course. Halfway home I produced a small bottle of bourbon from the back seat. "Would you like a drink, Don?"

He looked at the bottle in surprise.

"It's bourbon," I said.

"I know Jim Beam when I see it. How did you know it was my brand?

"It's your bottle," I replied. "It slid out from under the seat when I was driving your Buick." I poured him a couple of fingers in a small glass.

"To The Flying Circus" he said raising the drink. "An airline that serves bourbon on its flights will surely succeed. I'll recommend you to my friends."

17

Chapter Four

Let the big time roll

Don Hitchcock and I flew most Monday mornings and Friday evenings on the Toronto commute. On the way we wobbled through the lessons of the Private Pilot Licence: turns, climbs, descents, slow flight and stalls. At each destination, he careened through a couple of landings and go-arounds before I talked him to a full stop.

Don's progress was slow and unsteady. Part of his problem was learning to fly while balancing a coffee or bourbon in one hand and the control wheel in the other. We did eventually come to the point where, to receive a pilot licence, Don would have to pass a medical examination and fly solo.

"Did you book an appointment with one of those doctors on the list I gave you?" I asked on the way home one Friday.

Don was sawing away at the controls in slow flight. "If you were me, would you want to know your medical condition?" he asked with a laugh.

"The government wants to know before it will give you a pilot licence," I replied.

"My liver is none of the government's business," he said. "Did you bring the bourbon?"

I poured him a short drink, timing the glugs to match the rock and roll of his flying.

I didn't press the medical issue. If Don was content to fly to Toronto and back with me, that was fine but he was a restless guy. I couldn't imagine him chugging along in the Cherokee forever.

One Monday he asked, "If I buy an airplane, would you guys use it between my Monday and Friday flights?"

"Absolutely, Don," I replied quickly. "What do you have in mind?" I immediately conjured thoughts of boring holes in the sky in a high-powered aircraft with retractable landing gear and a panel full of electronics.

Maybe Henry and I could talk the jolly politician into a small, twin-engine speedster so we could really go after the charter market.

"I thought maybe something a little more exciting might spice up the ride to work," he replied. "It could add a different dimension to your flying school."

"Good idea," I said. "I'll talk to Henry about it."

That week, Henry and I discussed little else. We tried to speculate what kind of corporate aircraft our over-fed benefactor might agree to buy.

"An eight-passenger Piper Navajo would be perfect," I enthused.

"Remember," Henry cautioned, "he probably wants us to take care of the fixed costs. A Navajo would eat us alive. Besides, you still have to teach him how to fly."

"You're right. Maybe we should settle for an Aztec or a Seminole."

"A Twin Comanche would give us the speed for charter," Henry countered, "and we could still offer economical career training."

"OK, we'll talk to him at the end of the week."

I landed at the Toronto Island Airport at sunset that Friday. Don was already there. He was standing in front of the old passenger terminal next to a tall, skinny man in a trench coat. I recognized Skid Sicamore right away. He was an aircraft salesman from Derry. I mentally cringed. Sicamore had a well-earned reputation. He was high on slime and low on scruples. He was the last person I wanted to see talking to Don.

I shut down the engine and climbed onto the Cherokee's wing. Don came around the tail.

"Hi there, hotshot. I'd like you to meet Skid Sicamore."

"Ah, we've met before," I said jumping off the wing.

Skid knew that I knew his reputation. He gave me a nod but didn't offer a handshake. I returned the minimal greeting.

Don missed the snubs. His grin was extra wide. He gestured across the asphalt to the other side of the ramp. "So what do you think?"

My gaze followed his arm. It was pointing toward a small airplane sitting on a tailwheel-type landing gear. In the failing light, an unmistakable yellow and orange sunburst paint scheme appeared slightly faded on fabric covering.

"A Citabria?" I asked suspiciously.

"Our Citabria," Don replied excitedly. "Skid and I just closed the deal. Come on, have a look." He headed across the apron.

I glared at Skid.

"After you, 'hotshot'," he said with a smirk.

I followed Don. Citabrias are two-seat, high-wing, fabric-covered, aerobatic training airplanes. On the outside, this one looked better than

19

some of the derelicts that I had seen Skid peddle in the past. Don opened the single door on the right side. "Isn't she a beauty?" he declared, stepping back.

I ducked under the wing and walked behind the strut. The inside of the Citabria sported a basic utility look. Steel bracing tubes crisscrossed a sparsely upholstered cabin. A single communication radio sat forlornly in a nearly naked instrument panel. The airplane was as far from a charter or advanced training type as possible.

"Did you really buy this?" I asked. I didn't know what else to say.

"Yeah," Don answered excitedly. "Imagine the fun we'll have flitting to work in this baby. And you can teach aerobatics in it the rest of the time."

"Ah, it isn't exactly what Henry and I had in mind," I offered weakly.

Don wasn't listening. "We can loop all the way to Toronto and roll all the way home." He laughed and slapped me on the back. "Hop in. Skid's going to check you out right now. Henry can ride over with us on Monday and you can fly it back."

"Ah, it's getting dark, Don," I said.

"A couple of circuits should be all we need," Skid said from behind me. "I've already checked 'er over."

I could see no immediate escape but I had several concerns. I knew Skid's idea of a "check over" was less than I did before getting into a car. The wings could be falling off and he wouldn't know or care. My biggest fear was what Henry would think when he learned about Don's idea of a "corporate" airplane.

I hauled myself up with the brace in the windshield and dropped into the front seat. I had never flown a Citabria. The little airplane held two people sitting one behind the other bobsled style. It was controlled by sticks mounted in the floor ahead of the seats. The throttle was on the left windowsill. Below, by the pilot's left hip, was a panel with ignition switches, a carburetor heat control and pitch trim. While I was taking all this in, Sicamore squeezed past me into the back seat. On his way by, he pushed the mixture control in on the instrument panel. As he sat down, he leaned forward and flipped on the ignition.

"Be a good chap and punch the starter," he said pointing past my head to a button on the front panel. "Clear?" he called out to Don.

"I'll just put my seat belt on," I replied.

Sicamore flipped a set of broad belts off the floor into my lap and two more over my shoulders. "Here, figure these out while I taxi. Push the button."

Don was smiling and waving while backing away. I hit the starter. The engine caught and the airplane moved forward immediately.

"Turn the radio on, will ya?" Sicamore said.

"Be a good chap and punch the starter."

The communications microphone was mounted on the side panel above the left window. The aircraft salesman reached for it. I turned on the radio.

"Island Ground, Lima Oscar Oscar Papa taxi for a couple of circuits."

"Lima Oscar Oscar Papa, ground, Runway 28, wind calm, altimeter 29.98, taxi Charlie, Delta and turn your nav lights on."

"Hit the nav light switch up there buddy," Sicamore said to me. He didn't bother to acknowledge the controller's instructions.

I had the four-point harness figured out and on as we reached the beginning of the runway. Sicamore skipped the pre-take-off check.

"Switch the radio to tower, sonny," he barked.

I did.

"O P is ready for takeoff," Sicamore said into the microphone.

As the tower was giving us a take-off clearance, Sicamore gunned the throttle. The airplane squirted onto the runway.

"You have control," he announced.

I placed my right hand on the stick and my feet on the rudder pedals. As I reached for the throttle, Sicamore slammed it wide open from the back seat. The Citabria lurched forward and yawed left. I could feel Sicamore stabbing the right rudder. I moved the stick forward. The tail came up. I held it there while the aircraft accelerated, then I eased back. The airplane lifted off the runway.

The performance was not spectacular. This was either a small-engine Citabria or a very tired large-engine Citabria. Sicamore stayed quiet while I climbed us up to 1,000 feet and leveled off.

"When you turn downwind, I'll take it and show you some aerobatics," Sicamore said.

"Ah, that's not necessary, Skid," I said quickly. Aerobatics at 1,000 feet in failing light wasn't my idea of how to live a long life. "Aerobatics are not allowed in the control zone," I called out to the back seat. I turned downwind.

"I have control," Skid declared. "The airplane doesn't know it's night and the controller won't notice a loop if you turn the nav lights off for a minute."

The stick wiggled back and forth in my hand. Before I could speak or let go, Sicamore shoved the nose down and hit full power. I turned off the nav lights.

The engine roared and the wind shrieked through numerous cracks around the door and windows.

"You dive 'er to build up extra speed," the salesman declared. He had to yell to be heard.

When the airspeed indicator reached 120 mph, Sicamore hauled back on the stick. I was pressed in my seat as the nose shot skyward.

"You keep 'er straight with rudder," Sicamore continued to explain as the airplane slowed over the top of a loop. "Inverted is a good time to check the wings are level."

I thought it would be a miracle if Skid didn't fly us into Lake Ontario. The Island Airport is on the Toronto shoreline. The lights of the city lit up the horizon on our left but ahead and to the right was a gray hole.

The Citabria headed down the backside of the manoeuvre. Sicamore jerked the power to idle and pulled more gs as the speed increased again.

"Nav lights on," he commanded. "You have control."

I grabbed my stick. We had lost 200 feet during the manoeuvre. I flew level, completed a pre-landing check and turned toward the runway.

"O P turning base for a touch and go," Sicamore called into the microphone.

"Cleared touch and go Runway 28, Oscar Papa, wind two five zero at five."

There was no reply from the back seat. I reduced the power and set up an approach. There were no flaps so I just trimmed the nose to hold 80 mph and adjusted the power to descend to the runway. Sicamore said nothing but I could feel his hand on the stick. When I flared out, we floated down the runway quite a bit before touching down in a stall landing. I wiggled the rudder pedals to keep straight on the runway, then applied full power and took off again.

"Try a little less speed on the next approach," the back seat suggested over the noise of our full-power climb.

When I had leveled off on the downwind leg, Sicamore said, "Kill the nav lights and try a loop. Dive for speed and then pull the stick most of the way back."

I followed his instructions. I eased the nose down. Skid immediately shoved the throttle wide open. When the speed hit 120 mph, I pulled back on the stick.

"Harder!" the back seat yelled. I could feel his extra pull on the controls. "Right rudder!"

We were zooming toward a dark sky. There was no reference forward but I pushed the rudder anyway. The Citabria shuddered a bit as it staggered over the top of the loop. The lights of the Toronto skyline appeared inverted on the left side. We were crooked but before I could figure which way to correct with ailerons, Skid did it for me.

"Relax some back pressure," he barked.

I obeyed. The speed immediately started to build up.

Skid chopped the power. "Okay, pull 'er around."

I hauled back on the stick. The skyline reappeared right side up. I leveled off. We had lost 400 feet.

"Nav lights!" Skid called.

I flipped the lights on. Skid called the tower for a touch and go.

"Cleared touch and go Runway 28, Oscar Papa. Wind two six zero at five."

I turned the Citabria on a base leg and set up an approach at 75 mph. We touched down closer to the beginning of the runway. I applied full power and took off again. When we had reached 1,000 feet above ground,

I leveled off and turned parallel to the runway.

Skid yelled from the back seat and wiggled the stick, "I've got it."

I let go of the controls.

"I'll show you a roll," he said. "To keep the engine running upside-down, we'll do a barrel roll."

He dropped the nose to build up speed and then pulled it up to the horizon. The control stick slammed against my left leg. The Citabria slued around to the left. The lights of Toronto slued to the right. As we were passing inverted, the stick moved forward. When the skyline lights returned to their rightful places, Skid neutralized the controls.

"Oscar Papa, what's happening out there?" the controller asked.

We had forgotten to turn off the nav lights.

"Just some turn practice," Skid replied. "We're ready for another touch and go."

"Cleared touch and go," the controller replied. "If you're going to make excursions on the downwind, ask first."

Skid didn't reply.

I flew a touch and go. The airplane was starting to feel familiar.

When I turned downwind on the next circuit, Skid said, "Kill the nav lights and try a roll to the left."

I did, or at least we did. Skid did most of the work. I obviously wasn't responding fast enough. I was barely able to keep the stick in my hand. When the airplane came back around, Skid declared, "Well done!"

"A full stop this time for O P," he said into the microphone.

"I've lost contact with you Oscar Papa. Confirm you are on a base leg?"

"Nav lights!" Skid bellowed.

"Turning base now," he said into the microphone.

I turned the lights on.

"Cleared to land, Runway 28, Oscar Papa. Wind calm."

I flew to a landing and taxied in. Skid directed me to park over by a hangar. He opened the door and started climbing out before I had shut down the engine.

"Good flying, hotshot," he barked into my ear. "Enjoy your corporate airplane."

Chapter Five

The Chipmunk Challenge

Don's strange choice of a business airplane disappointed me but did not discourage Henry. It helped that the easy-going customer offered us a generous lease. He would cover all fixed and operating expenses on the Citabria. The Flying Circus would pay him a low-dollar figure per revenue flying hour with no minimum time. I still had my heart set on a real corporate airplane.

"The deal guarantees us a profit whenever we fly it," Henry said optimistically. We were drinking coffee in the office early one morning.

"I don't care what it doesn't cost us," I complained. "Businessmen won't charter a drafty, slow, two-seat, rag-covered airplane."

"Then we'll sell tailwheel check-outs to our pilot customers."

"OK, but after we run through those five or six people, what do we do?"

"Well, no other school around here offers aerobatic lessons."

The idea held some appeal. I had flown some aerobatics before, not counting my night-fright with Skid Sicamore.

"Neither of us has an Aerobatic Endorsement on our Instructor Ratings," I replied.

Henry reached behind the counter and pulled out a book. It was a copy of "Roll-around-a-point" by Duane Cole.

"Here's everything you need to know," he said, handing me the book. "I could learn, but you're the one with aerobatic experience and you'll be flying the Citabria with Don."

I looked at the cover. It pictured a Taylorcraft flying upside down. I knew Cole was famous for his tight airshow routine in the underpowered little taildragger.

"I'm interested but teaching aerobatics is not something you learn from a book," I replied, flipping through the pages.

"I agree," Henry answered. "That's why I talked to Ben Ivory. He'd be happy to give you an endorsement course in his Chipmunk."

"You're kidding!" I exclaimed in surprise.

"Actually, this time I'm not," he laughed.

Ben Ivory was a local funeral director who had learned to fly on de Havilland Tiger Moths and Chipmunks in the air force. He went on to be a career fighter pilot before retiring to the family business in Circus.

When the air force decommissioned its Chipmunks, Ben bought one.

He stored it in the flying club hangar across the ramp from The Flying Circus. Henry and I often saw him departing early in the morning for an hour of aerobatics in the sleek metal trainer. The prospect of learning from Ben was exciting.

"I've never seen him fly with anyone," I said. "I thought he never gave rides or instruction."

"I asked him about that," Henry replied. "He said when he pushes the Chipmunk out, pilots admire it but no one has asked to go up."

"Maybe they've seen how he tortures his airplane on takeoff," I suggested with a chuckle.

Ben's takeoffs were always spectacular. He'd line up with the runway centreline and apply full power. The Chipmunk's tail would come up and he would accelerate to flying speed. Then Ben lifted the main wheels six inches off the asphalt and held them there all the way to the end of the runway. At that point he'd haul the stick back into a zoom climb almost straight up. When Ben had gone as high as the 145-hp engine would take him, he'd level off and turn toward the practice area.

"He suggested that you read Cole's book and then call him for a lesson."

"Wow, that's fantastic! What a nice guy!"

"He asked if you'd lost any weight."

"Oh, oh. That means he's going to wring me out."

"Well, if you'd rather not do this, I will," Henry smiled.

"Not a chance. If I can stay conscious, I'll learn more about aerobatics from Ben than anyone else."

Chapter Six

Egress, egress, egress

B en Ivory did not look like a funeral director. We met at the flying club hangar early in the morning. He was wearing a one-piece flight suit from his air force days. It still fit after 20 years. Ben was medium height and trim. He reminded me of an older high school gym teacher who started each day with one-armed push-ups.

Ben had the cowling open on the left side of his Chipmunk and was checking the engine. He turned as I approached. The lines creasing Ben's face and the gray in his hair gave a hint of his age but his eyes and stance were fighter-pilot firm. I wasn't sure if I should salute him or shake his hand. Since the only salute I knew was scout's honour, I accepted his handshake.

"Good to see you again," he said warmly but crisply.

"Thank you," I replied. "I really appreciate your offer to run me through the aerobatics endorsement."

"Happy to help. Actually, I'm looking forward to it. It's been too long since I've taught anyone."

With that, he turned toward the engine and continued his pre-flight inspection. "I'll finish the walkaround and then we'll be ready to go."

The Chipmunk was designed and built by de Havilland in Canada. The air force flew them as a basic trainer during the 1950s. The instructor and student sat one behind the other under a single bubble canopy.

Ben's Chipmunk sat on its tailwheel, looking too small and graceful to be military. It was not painted. The bare aluminum was polished to a brilliant shine. The only visual break was a white band around the fuselage behind the canopy that carried an air force squadron insignia.

"We'll cover the basic aerobatic manoeuvres until you've mastered them," he said, "and then we'll do unusual attitude recoveries."

I realized as he spoke that my lesson had started. I followed him around the airplane.

"You have to be prepared for anything when teaching aerobatics," he continued. "Student pilots can invent strange manoeuvres in their excitement. You need to follow what's happening and know how to recover."

"It sounds interesting," I replied dutifully.

He turned and looked at me. "Of course it helps to be in good physical condition. It's not easy to withstand the rigors of the students' gyrations."

"Yes sir," I replied. "I've been dieting since I spoke to you on Tuesday."

Ben returned a slight smile at my little joke. Then he gave my stomach a poke. "You'll need more than a two-day diet."

I had already decided that nothing could bother me after the night tumbling lesson with Skid Sicamore. This mild-mannered funeral director could not be worse.

"I don't think the aerobatics will be a problem," I offered.

"We'll see."

Ben finished the walkaround and pointed toward the far side of the airplane. "If you take the other wingtip, we'll push her out."

The Chipmunk was light and easy to move on the ramp. In the sunshine, the swirls in the polished aluminum were dazzling.

Ben climbed onto the left wing, slid the canopy open and hauled out two parachutes. He jumped down and showed me how to strap one on. A hefty harness on my front held reinforced canvas to my back. The actual parachute was a seat pack that dangled over my behind.

Ben strapped the other chute on and hopped onto the wing. He motioned for me to join him. "You ride in the instructor seat in the back."

I climbed up. The two cockpits looked cramped and sparse. There was no upholstery. The seats were bare aluminum. The control sticks growing out of the floor were each capped with a leather flying helmet.

Under Ben's direction, I carefully hoisted a leg over the high sill and stepped onto the back seat. Then I wiggled the other leg in and lowered myself until I was sitting on the parachute. My body filled the rear cockpit. It felt like I had put the airplane on like an old overcoat rather than climbing into it.

Ben had hung my shoulder belts over the canopy rails. Now he squatted beside me and draped one over each shoulder.

"You'll find the lap harnesses on the floor," he said.

I leaned forward and dug around until I came up with two heavy belts.

"There's one more that goes between your legs," he said patiently.

When I had found it, Ben showed me how to snap all the ends into a single round buckle. By the time I was done, I felt like the Michelin man in a straight jacket. I was getting warm.

"We should not need to exit this airplane in the air," he offered calmly, "but just in case, I'll explain the drill. First I shout, 'Egress, egress, egress!' Then I'll release the canopy. The windblast will be loud and buffeting. That's when you release your harness like this."

Ben twisted the knob on my chest. The five belts fell away.

"Next, I'll roll the airplane inverted if I can. You'll fall out. I'll follow. Count to three and pull this," he said tapping on a D-shaped metal ring over my heart. "The parachute will do the rest."

I hadn't figured on an introduction to skydiving as part of this lesson but I kept that thought to myself. I started to sweat under the rising autumn sun.

Ben refastened my harness. "If I can't roll us over, don't wait," he continued, "climb onto the wing and jump. Try it now."

"You want me to jump out now?"

"Yes," he replied, stepping out of my way. "Release your harness, climb onto the wing and jump onto the ground but don't pull the D-ring."

By now, a small crowd had gathered on the ramp. This happened whenever Ben wheeled out the Chipmunk. I assumed it was the attraction of seeing the most interesting airplane on the airport.

I released the harness buckle without any problem, placed the belts to the side and struggled to my feet. Then I climbed onto my seat and hoisted first one leg and then the other onto the wingwalk. The exertion left me wobbling on the slanted wing. I jumped off the trailing edge of the wing onto the ground and fell over with a thump of canvas and the rattle of buckles.

I slowly picked myself up. Ben spoke from his perch beside the front cockpit. "That's the idea but you'll save time by ignoring the seat belts once they're released and then hopping rather than climbing out."

I stood there for a moment feeling pain arrive to my scraped hands and places where the parachute buckles had dug in.

"Yes sir," I replied. Sweat was trickling from my armpits.

"Try it once more," Ben added calmly.

I couldn't believe it. This man must enjoy watching people hurt themselves, I thought. I gave him a sour look. "You want me to do that over again?"

"Yes," he replied. "It would be bad enough to lose the airplane but I'd feel worse if it crashed with you still in it."

It was easy to picture Ben as a tough air force instructor. I decided that I had two choices: I could undo the parachute and walk away or I could do as he said. At least I was putting smiles on the faces of the bystanders.

I hoisted myself onto the wing and into the cockpit. Then I fished out the seat belts and snapped them together. My clothes were now soaking with sweat. I took a deep breath.

"Try it once more."

"Whenever you're ready," Ben said.

I unlocked the harness. Pushing as hard as I could with my arms and legs, I tried to explode out of the cockpit. My feet cleared the seat but not the canopy rail. I crashed head and shoulders first, onto the wing. When I unhooked my feet, I rolled unceremoniously off the wing onto the ground.

I turned and looked up at Ben through sweat stained eyes.

"That'll do it," he declared. "Let's go flying."

Chapter Seven

Where's the bag?

I picked myself off the pavement. Ben didn't wait. He hopped into the front cockpit and settled onto the seat. I decided he'd leave without me if I didn't keep going. By now I had invested enough pain and embarrassment in this lesson, I was determined to go. I hauled myself onto the wing and into the rear seat once more.

Ben yelled, "Clear?" and hit the starter. The propeller turned twice and the engine coughed to life. We rolled forward immediately.

I found my seat belts, sorted them as best I could and latched them together. The propwash on my face felt good but it wasn't penetrating the canvas web covering my wet clothes.

Ben taxied the Chipmunk to the edge of the ramp and swung it around. He held up his leather helmet indicating I should put mine on. I picked it up from the control stick. There were earphones in little leather pockets on each side of the helmet. Rubber tubes ran from them forward under the instrument panel. The tubes looked like they were borrowed from a doctor's stethoscope. A similar tube ran from a mouthpiece that was dangling from the helmet. I found out later that they were gosport tubes, an early communication device for air force instructors and students.

I lifted the helmet over my head. Ben chose that moment to run up the engine with the brakes on. The canopy was still open. I managed not to lose anything in the propeller blast but I was pummeled in the face by the helmet for my trouble. When Ben finally reduced the power, I was holding a twisted puzzle of leather and rubber.

I unraveled the mess as Ben finished his pre-take-off checks and taxied out. To use the entire 5,000 feet of runway, he had to backtrack from the mid-point. By the time the airplane was in position to go, I had the helmet on and was clipping the mouthpiece across my face.

I heard him in my headset. It sounded like he was at the other end of a long sewer pipe. "Ready to pull some gs?" he asked enthusiastically.

I held the mouthpiece against my lips. "Yes, sir," I yelled.

"OK," he answered in a raised voice, "but you don't have to shout."

"Yes sir," I said quietly.

"That's better. Now slide the canopy forward and I'll close it."

I stretched my right arm behind me and pulled the canopy rim toward Ben until he could reach back for it.

Next I could hear him call the control tower. "Foxtrot Lima India Papa ready for takeoff with a pull-up."

I tried to relax as I pictured Ben's standard high-g departures. My helmet was not rigged to receive the radio replies so the next thing I heard was Ben smoothly applying full power. The Chipmunk squirted ahead easily. Ben brought the tail up and accelerated until the main wheels lifted off. Then he eased the stick forward. The engine rpm wound up as the speed increased. We could have been climbing before the halfway point of the runway but Ben held the Chipmunk level. We accelerated for the whole 5,000 feet. The tail got so high, I could see over Ben's head to the fence off the end of the runway.

"The trick with aerobatics in a basic trainer," Ben calmly announced through the tube, "is to be firm but smooth."

He hauled back on the control stick. The Chipmunk shot skyward. The down force was so strong my stomach tried to fit itself into my boots. It seemed to last a long time. I looked up and could see nothing but blue sky. I felt dizzy and disoriented.

"In high g manoeuvres," Ben advised, "clench your stomach muscles so all your blood doesn't leave your head."

Now he tells me, I thought.

"I love the pull of gs in the morning," Ben mused in my earphones.

He pushed the stick forward as I was trying to tighten my stomach. The little airplane arched from the vertical to level flight. I floated against my shoulder harness. Now I felt light-headed as well as dizzy and disoriented.

"You have control," Ben declared.

I was too confused to protest. I grabbed the control stick between my legs and looked forward. The horizon was steady but my head was swimming. My hand followed my head and so did the airplane. The controls in the Chipmunk were sensitive. We wobbled through the sky while I tried to hold the horizon level. I let go of the stick, put my head down and took a deep breath.

"Sorry Ben," I said, as my head began to clear, "the pull-up caught me off guard."

"Ex-military aircraft take off like that automatically," he chuckled cheerfully. "They don't know how to make conventional departures."

I started to feel a little better. "I bet that goes for ex-military pilots too," I replied.

"All the good ones," he laughed. "It looks like you're getting the hang of it now."

I lifted my head. The Chipmunk was flying itself perfectly straight and level.

"Take us to the practice area," Ben said, "and we'll have some fun."

I placed one finger on top of the stick and guided the Chipmunk away from the airport. During the interlude my body parts had time to find their rightful places. I started to enjoy the airplane's responsive controls and the spectacular all-around view through the bubble canopy.

"I have control," Ben announced as he wiggled the stick. "We'll start with a loop. I'll show you the first one."

He commenced turns each way to check for other air traffic. I took a deep breath and tried to clench my stomach muscles.

"We'll line up with a road for a reference," he continued, rolling the airplane out of a turn. "Then we need some extra speed."

Ben eased the Chipmunk's nose down until I could see we were lined up on a straight country road.

"At 120 mph, we pitch up smoothly but firmly."

He moved the stick back. The Chipmunk followed. We inscribed a graceful arch upward. The extra g force made me feel like I was wearing a cement suit.

The cruise power setting was enough to haul the little airplane over the top. As we swung down the backside, Ben reduced the power and eased out of the dive. At the bottom of the loop, I could see we were still in line with the road. Ben continued curving to a slight nose-up attitude to regain lost altitude.

"Student practice," he announced through the tubes.

Wiggling the stick, I replied, "I have control."

I tried to relax while flying clearing turns in each direction. The Chipmunk's controls were wonderfully light.

I lined up on a road and set up a shallow dive. At 120 mph, I hauled back on the stick and immediately discovered two things about the Chipmunk. The British-built Gypsy Major engine rotated in the opposite direction to North American engines. During the pitch-up, the Chipmunk yawed right instead of left. I wasn't ready for it.

About the same time, I realized that the controls were more effective than on any aircraft I had flown. I had pulled too hard on the stick. The airplane shuddered as it approached a high-speed stall. Then the world rotated around me. The yaw combined with the wing stall forced the Chipmunk into a snap roll to the left.

I didn't know what to do so I just held onto the stick. Ben wasn't saying anything.

"Now what?" I yelped as the airplane started its third corkscrew.

"You got us in," he replied calmly. "You recover."

The Chipmunk's nose was dropping as we approached the fourth gyration to the left. The road ahead rotated right. We were falling into a spin. I applied right rudder and eased the stick forward. The airplane stopped spinning and pointed its nose straight down. I reduced the power and pulled out of the dive.

"That's it," Ben said enthusiastically. "Now use the extra speed to regain some altitude."

"Yes sir," I replied weakly and eased into a climb.

During previous aerobatic flying I had ridden in the front seat. I didn't appreciate that it was on the rotational axis. The rear seat was behind the axis where every gyration was exaggerated. That combined with my previous exertions and the hothouse effect of the sun shining through the Plexiglas was making me feel nauseated for the first time in my flying career.

"That last one was a student mistake we were going to cover later," Ben declared. "Now we don't have to, but you still haven't done a loop. Go ahead when ready."

"Yes sir."

I set up for the manoeuvre again. This time I took it easy on the pitch-up and remembered left rudder to counteract the engine rotation. The Chipmunk obediently arched skyward. Everything seemed to be going well until we were reaching the top. I hadn't pulled hard enough on the stick. The wings stalled when we were inverted. The Chipmunk tumbled into a spin to the left which I didn't recognize immediately.

"Student mistake number two," Ben declared as the airplane twirled earthward. He didn't do anything about it or offer any advice.

I figured things out by the third rotation and initiated a spin recovery.

"You should have it now. Try the loop again."

I was feeling woozier with each botched manoeuvre but I was determined not to let on to Ben. I started another loop. This time the little airplane sailed all the way around. It felt good to complete one but I was still feeling unsteady. Maybe the lesson will end soon, I said to myself. I looked around for sick bags.

"That wasn't a loop," Ben exclaimed from the front seat. "Loops are round. You have to adjust the amount of pitch control to match the changing speed as you go up and come down. Try it again."

I flew another one. Coming over the top of the loop, I could feel the nose tucking in where the speed was the slowest so I eased off my pressure on the stick. The speed picked up immediately. I had to pull hard to prevent us from going into a screaming dive.

"That was a square," Ben announced impatiently. "I have control."

The stick wiggled in my hand. I let go. I couldn't find any sick sacks.

"I'll show you another one," Ben continued. He turned slightly left and then right to look for traffic and then lined up on a road. "You have to be smooth," he instructed as he dipped the Chipmunk's nose to gain speed.

This time I watched the movement of my control stick. Ben pulled it back. The Chipmunk went up and my stomach went down. The control movements from there were tiny; a little forward, a little back, then to neutral as we regained level flight. I looked up. My head started to spin. A sour taste gurgled up from my stomach. I took a deep breath and swallowed hard a couple of times.

"Now you do one like that," Ben said cheerfully.

I decided that Ben may have been the world's best pilot but he was a lousy instructor. He wanted me to fly a round loop without telling me how or describing it in his demonstrations.

"I have control," I said as I fought back nausea. I groped for the stick and wobbled it.

"Let me know before you're going to be sick," he said casually.

"I'm fine," I replied weakly.

"Not likely. Your breath coming through the voice tube would stop a team of run-away horses. Try one more loop and then we'll head for the barn."

"Yes sir."

"Let me know before you're going to be sick."

36

I banked the wings pretending to look for traffic but I kept my head down most of the time. I pushed the stick forward briefly, clenched my stomach muscles and pulled back without looking outside. The airplane pitched up and over the top. I had no idea if the wings were level and I didn't care. On the back half of the manoeuvre, I worked the stick back and forth more or less like Ben had. As the speed increased I looked up long enough to see when I should level off. My stomach protested loudly.

"Now you've got the idea," Ben declared. "I have control." He wiggled the stick out of my hand and entered a turn. I was hopeful that it was toward the airport.

"I'll show you another manoeuvre on the way back," he said. With that he flicked the Chipmunk into a roll to the right. The horizon rotated the other way. He stopped it precisely upside down.

My stomach churned. Ben rolled left all the way around and stopped us inverted again. My stomach boiled. Then the ex-fighter pilot rolled us right side up.

I could feel that my breakfast had reached the point of return. I didn't want to open my mouth to tell Ben because I knew it would not be words coming out.

"Smelling pretty bad from back there," Ben said. "I'll fly no-barf turns to the airport. You unclip your mask so I don't have to share your breakfast."

I had never heard of a "no-barf" turn but I soon learned what it was. I undid the snaps on my mask while Ben placed the Chipmunk into a tight turn to the left. Constantly pulling two gs or more, he shaped the turns so that we were working our way slowly back to the airport. I could hear him call Circus Tower and request a "circles" approach. I was feeling very sick. I was willing him to stop the rotating and just get us on the ground when I realized that the stupid manoeuvre was working. As bad as I felt, the extra pressure on my stomach kept me from throwing up.

Closer to the runways, Ben added a descent to our continuous turning. Our last revolution was over the runway. From there we spiraled into a landing. As soon as we touched down, he slid the canopy open. The blast of fresh air felt good.

Ben turned off the runway and did a fast taxi to the ramp. As soon as he had shut the engine down in front of the hangar, he hoped out, turned toward me and started undoing my seat harness.

"I'm fine," I lied. I just wanted to sit still until my stomach settled down.

"Sure," Ben replied, "and I'm the King of Prussia. You'll be fine but not for a while. In the meantime, I'd feel better if you weren't sitting in my airplane waiting for an eruption." He practically lifted me onto the wingwalk himself. "I'll help you down," he said.

So much for getting an aerobatic endorsement, I thought to myself. Mr. Macho Pilot would probably not allow me in his aircraft again. That was OK. Getting sick was no fun even though the only permanent damage was to my ego.

"When are you available for lesson number two?" Ben asked when we were on the ramp unbuckling our parachutes.

"I didn't do so well on this one," I replied lamely.

"Nonsense. In all my years of aerobatics no one has lasted with me as long as you. I couldn't believe someone that out-of-shape would set a new record. How about another lesson tomorrow?"

"How about next Tuesday?" I countered. I wanted to see how long it would take my head and stomach to recover. "That will give me more time to practise my one-armed push-ups."

"Same time next Tuesday it is," he grinned. "You should practise those stomach clenches too."

"Yes sir."

Chapter Eight

Flight to nowhere

My morning aerobatic workouts with Ben Ivory continued. I fared better by eating less breakfast and wearing lighter clothes. The old air force colonel became friendlier as the challenge to make me sick wore off. Between lessons I practised what I had learned in the Citabria.

In the meantime Henry promoted our fledgling charter business in the local newspaper. I answered the phone the day a man called about a flight.

"This is Olaf Petterson," he announced slowly and with authority. He had a rough voice. "Don Hitchcock said you could fly me to my construction site up north."

"Yes sir, we can," I answered quickly. I was determined to make up for my dozy response to our first charter call. I pulled out a copy of the form that Henry had prepared and wrote down the man's name.

"Where is the site, Mr. Petterson?"

"It's 70 miles north of Sudbury," the customer replied, "about 50 miles west of New Liskeard and 70 miles south of Timmins."

I followed his directions with my finger on the chart that Henry had mounted on the wall.

"According to our map," I replied with hesitation, "there is nothing there."

"That's the place," Petterson replied confidently. "We're building a road there. I want to visit the site."

"Do you have someone who can pick you up at the Sudbury Airport?"

"I don't want to go to Sudbury," he said patiently. "I want to see the job and come right back."

"So you want to fly over the site and come back?"

"Flying over is good," he said a little less patiently, "and I want to land, walk around and talk to my men."

"So we'll be flying over the site and landing at the nearest airport?"

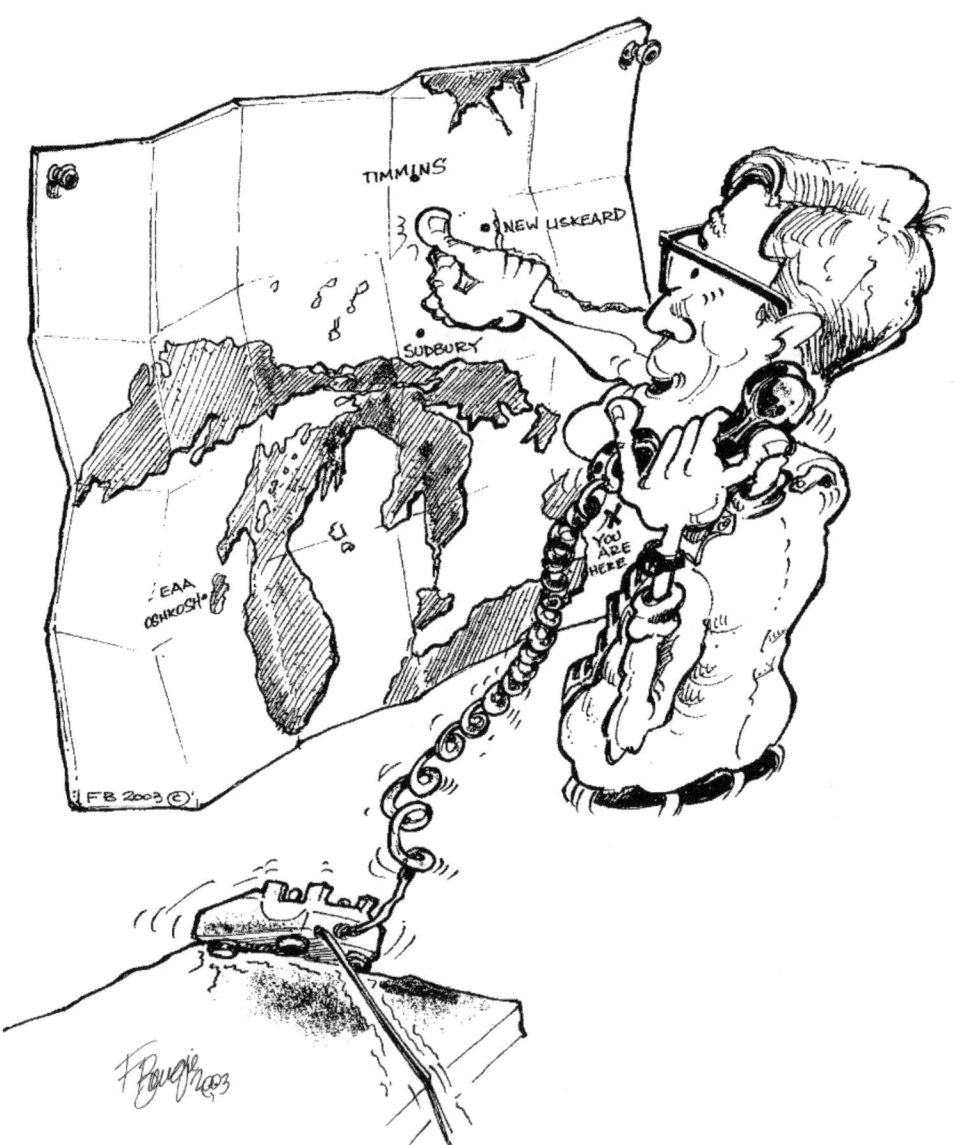

"According to our map there's nothing there."

"You can land at the nearest airport but I want to land at the job."

"Land at the site?"

"Yes!" Petterson declared.

"Ah... Mr., ah..." I looked at the name I had written down, "Petterson. We don't have a helicopter."

"We're building a road. Can't we land an airplane on the road?"

I pictured a northern road construction site as a narrow strip blasted and filled through alternating rock and swamp. Dozers and dumpers rocked and rolled over undulating piles of stone, dirt and gravel.

"Ah, I wouldn't want to commit to landing an airplane on the job site," I said hesitantly. "We'd have to take you to the nearest airport."

"No thanks," he grunted, and hung up.

I told Henry about the call when I saw him later. "I couldn't see us dropping a Cherokee on a raw construction site littered with road-building equipment," I explained. "So I told him we couldn't do it."

"What did he say?" Henry asked.

"He hung up."

"Do you have his phone number?"

"No. I knew we couldn't help him."

"Well, I'm thinking that the Citabria would be perfect."

I blushed. He was right and I hadn't thought of it. The Citabria had a high wing and tail-wheel landing gear that kept the propeller well clear of the ground. Henry was from the west where road landings in small planes were a way of life.

"Did you get the man's name?" my partner asked.

"Yes, Petterson." I held up the charter form.

"That would be Petterson Construction," Henry said. "I'll call him."

I listened while Henry called the man. He introduced himself and explained that we had the use of a different airplane that might be suitable for the flight. He filled me in on the other side of the conversation afterward.

"How long of a straight stretch of road do you have?" Henry asked.

"We're building it. How long do you want?" Petterson replied.

"Ah... we'll need half a mile clear of obstacles including wires."

"How wide?"

Henry told me that he mentally took the wing span of the Citabria and doubled it. "Seventy feet," he said.

"Good. I'll tell the boys to go straight for the next half mile. Should be ready Thursday. How's your schedule?"

"Thursday is good. Do you want me to land on the road in front of your house to pick you up?" he asked jokingly.

"That's a good idea," Petterson replied. "It's straight enough but it'll be dark. I want to leave at seven in the morning. Pick me up at Gravely

Air Park. It's not far away."

"OK," Henry replied. "I'll see you at the air park at seven unless the weather's bad. What's your home number in case we have to postpone?"

"Call this number. I live at the construction yard. My office is in the back of the house and the phone rings through."

"Fine. I'll see you at seven if I don't call by six-fifteen."

He hung up the phone and then looked at me. My eyes must have been wide. "What?"

"I have this vision of you lining up to land on a seventy-five-foot-wide slot blasted through a rock outcrop or on a ribbon of gravel snaking through bush or swamp."

Henry grinned. "No sweat. If it's not good enough, we won't land."

"OK. Whatever you say," I leaned over the counter to see whose name he was writing in the booking sheet as the pilot, "as long as it's your flight."

"I wouldn't miss it," he replied.

Chapter Nine

Road warriors

Henry departed The Flying Circus to pick up Olaf Petterson on Thursday before I arrived at work. He was gone all day.

That evening I waited in the office after flying with my last student. I expected a phone call announcing that my partner had bent the Citabria on its first revenue flight.

The sun was setting when I heard Henry on the office radio monitor. He was telling the Circus Control Tower that he was inbound for a landing. I met him on the ramp when he taxied in. He shut down the engine and opened the door.

"How'd it go?" I asked.

I had learned long ago that Henry was a word economist. To find out anything from him, I had to ask. My partner believed that people liked talking more than listening so he rarely volunteered information. It drove his wife nuts.

"Fine," he replied as he climbed out. He sounded bushed.

"I saw the wings as you were taxiing in," I said, tongue in cheek. "They look three to four feet shorter."

He glanced at the left wing and then smiled. "You wish."

Henry filled me in while we refueled the Citabria.

"I picked Petterson up at Gravely Air Park. By the way, he's one well-fed Viking. I'm sure we'll get more trips from him. If you're flying, don't let him take a lot of stuff or you'll never get airborne."

"Does he wear a helmet with horns on it?" I joked.

"No, lots of hair but no helmet," Henry replied. "So we flew all the way to the job site without refueling. I wanted to take off from the road as light as possible."

"Wow, how long was the flight?"

"Three and a half hours each way."

If Clouds Could Talk

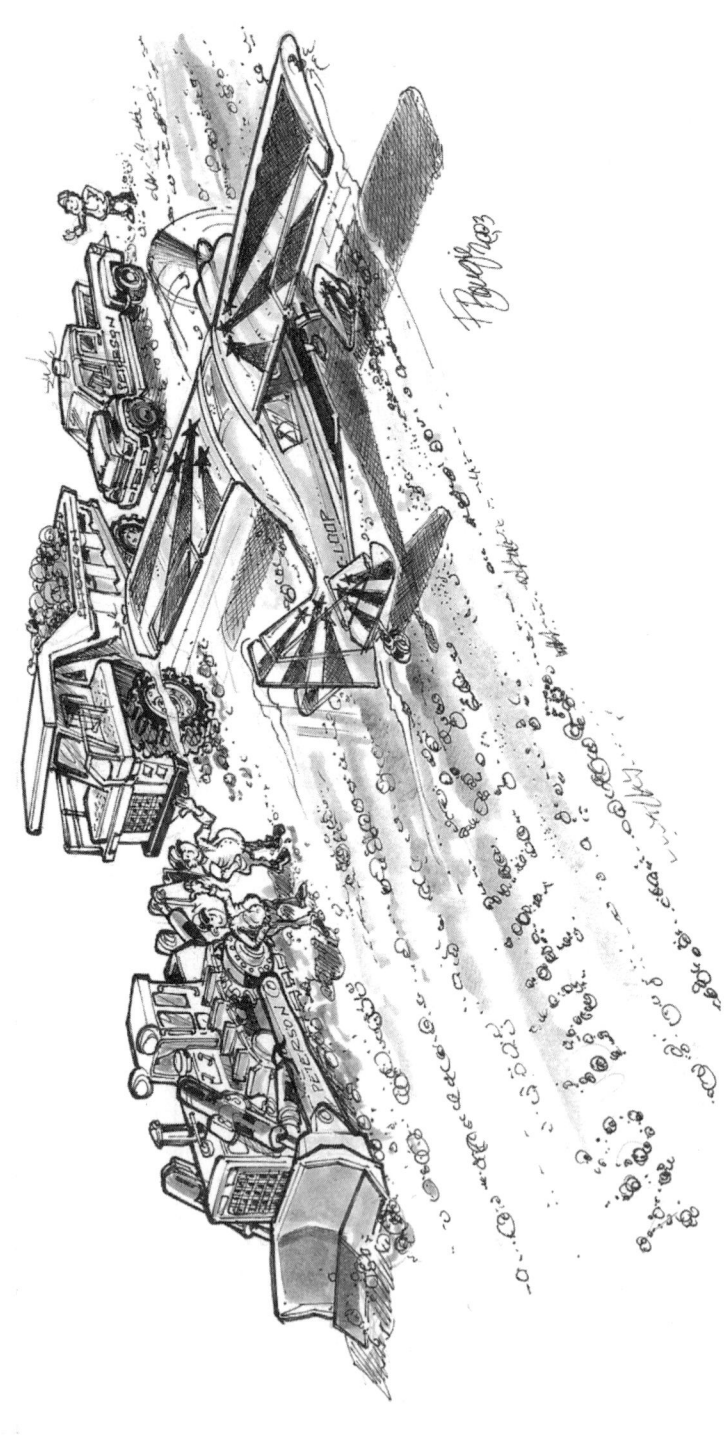

I winced. Seven hours folded into the Citabria would be crippling. "Well you had a good break at the job site. You've been gone 14 hours."

"Not really but I'll get to that in a minute."

Henry continued while we pushed the airplane into the hangar. "When we arrived overhead, his crews were finishing a straight stretch for us through the bush. It was compacted gravel, sand and dirt."

"No pavement?"

"No, but it was hard and smooth. They had even added a little turn-around for us before the next curve. Olaf had me fly up and down the site a couple of miles each way so he could see it before landing. By the time I lined up with the runway, the trucks and graders had pulled off to the left side. It looked like an honour guard of construction equipment saluting the boss."

"You landed with equipment parked on the side of the strip?"

"Sure. There was lots of room. When it's finished, that's going to be the best half-mile of road in the north. It'll make a perfect landing strip in an emergency."

Henry started cleaning dirt and bugs off the Citabria's windshield. I wiped down the leading edges of the wings and struts.

"We landed with no problem. Olaf joked that we only used 1,500 feet and wasted the rest. The job foreman, Rocky, met us at the turnaround and helped me pull Olaf out of the Citabria's back seat. They sat in a pick-up truck and went over the plans for the next section of construction. I talked to the workers who stopped to have a look at the airplane.

"A few minutes later, Olaf called me over and asked if I could fly Rocky to give him a bird's-eye view of the job site. I told them I only had enough fuel to make it back to Sudbury.

"They volunteered gas from their tanker but it was diesel so they drained car gas from Rocky's truck. I strained it through a rag. We need to take clean rags next time. Anyway, the flagmen stopped the equipment again and Rocky and I took off. We flew several passes ahead of the job and landed again. Olaf was waiting with three more guys and more gas. Two were surveyors and one was the dynamite man. Olaf asked if I could fly them too."

"No wonder you were gone so long."

"That wasn't all," Henry grinned. "By the time Olaf and I departed for Sudbury and home, I had flown ten more guys. They had drained three pick-up trucks dry. I've flown eleven hours revenue today."

"Wow, way to go!"

"Yeah, but I'm beat. Let's head home."

"Sure, but I was hoping since it's so late that you'd fly with Dan Ivory for me at dawn tomorrow."

"Not a chance."

Chapter Ten

One over Doomer

Ben Ivory and I flew ten hours of aerobatic lessons. We became friends. I admired his skill at making the Chipmunk dance. He appreciated my ability to ride the back seat without losing my cookies.

"Who does the government flight tests these days?" he asked when he was signing my application for an Aerobatic Endorsement.

"It's usually Inspector Kennedy," I replied.

"Doomer Kennedy?"

"I've heard him called that." The Inspector Kennedy I knew had a reputation for failing more than his share of flight test candidates and being miserable while doing it.

"I instructed a 'Doomer Kennedy' in the air force," Ben mused. "He barfed on every takeoff."

"How did he get the name 'Doomer'?"

"From his sour looks and his bad luck. He marched around the base with a scowl on his face and every time he flew, it seemed the airplane had some kind of problem. On a solo practice flight, his Chipmunk caught fire. He was afraid to bail out so he rode the burning plane to the ground. He received second degree burns to his legs. After that he was afraid of parachutes and fire."

"It must be the same guy," I said. I had flown with Kennedy on previous flight tests. Each one became memorable for what had gone wrong.

Ben handed me the completed application. "There, that should bring back memories for him," he chuckled.

I looked at Ben's signature. It read, "Col. Benjamin 'Flip' Ivory, (retired)." Below, he had written, "Hi Doomer, many happy returns."

"He'll know what I mean," Ben laughed. "Good luck with your test," he added, delivering an iron handshake. "It's been fun flying with you."

I went back to The Flying Circus office and booked a government flight test for ten days later. I practised in the Citabria over the next week. On the appointed day, I had the airplane cleaned and ready. It was sitting on the ramp complete with parachutes borrowed from Ben.

Inspector Kennedy walked through the office door shortly after nine o'clock. He was wearing a gray business suit and a worse-than-usual frown.

"Good morning sir," I said smartly.

He glanced at me quickly and headed to our briefing tables without saying anything. I followed. When we were sitting down, he leaned toward me and spoke in a low voice.

"I don't enjoy these aerobatic flight tests," he said sternly.

"Yes, sir," I replied politely, and I know why, I thought to myself.

"I find that the candidates don't have sufficient training and practice. Often their instructors have flown little more aerobatic time than they have."

"Yes, sir."

"Most of them fail," the granite-faced inspector continued, "but in the meantime I have to fly with them."

"I hope I don't let you down, sir," I replied in the most serious tone I could muster.

"Right, then," he said leaning back and speaking normally, "let me see your application."

I handed him the document in triplicate. He lifted his head to centre his bifocals on the top of the page.

One eyebrow went up. "It says you have ten hours of aerobatic instruction and 15 hours practice. How much of that is pen time?"

The man was accusing me of padding my log book with false entries. I could feel the blood rise in my neck.

"None, sir," I replied with a forced calmness. It was true. The 15 hours counted my previous aerobatic experience including the half-hour with Skid Sicamore.

"In the air force you would have had 40 hours of aerobatic instruction and more than that in the classroom," he snorted.

"Of course, sir."

His expression changed when he read the signature at the bottom. "You flew with Colonel Ivory?"

"Yes, sir."

"When was that?" he demanded. It sounded as if he didn't believe me.

"Last week was our last flight," I replied.

"One flight?"

"No, I did all ten hours dual with Ben... I mean the colonel."

"Colonel Ivory was the best aerobatic pilot in the air force," Kennedy said proudly. His tone questioned why such a great man would have anything to do with me.

"Yes, sir. The colonel retired to the family business here in Circus. He instructed me in his private Chipmunk."

Kennedy stared at the signature without saying anything for at least a minute. Finally he looked up. Unfriendliness returned to his face.

"Right," he said crisply, "let's get started. Pretend I have had the basic aerobatic lessons. Teach me how to recover from a tailslide."

I had read that this was a difficult manoeuvre. The elevator had the opposite effect when the airplane was sliding backward.

"Tailslides are prohibited in the Citabria," I announced hopefully.

"I don't want to fly one," Kennedy replied with a threatening scowl. "I want you to teach me the ground briefing."

I tried a new tactic. "The colonel never gave ground briefings," I offered. "He said that students learn best by flying."

"Yes, I'm sure he did," Kennedy replied. "Colonel Ivory may have been the best aerobatic pilot in the air force, but I'm the inspector."

"Yes, sir."

I delivered an awkward description of an awkward manoeuvre that I had never flown.

Without commenting, Kennedy said, "Now show me a ground briefing on entering and recovering from left and right-hand inverted flat spins."

Oh sure, I thought to myself. Inverted flat spin recoveries were the hardest thing to describe.

"The Citabria is not certified for inverted spins either," I declared.

It was true. The airplane was not built to withstand much negative g force. Ben and I had discussed inverted spins on the ground but he said he never flew them in his Chipmunk.

"I didn't say we were going to do inverted spins in the air. I want a ground briefing. Can you give me the pre-flight lesson on inverted flat spins or not?"

"Yes, sir."

I realized that Kennedy was either trying to fail me or extend the briefing until there was no time to fly. I started to describe the entry and recovery from an inverted spin using a model airplane.

"If the inverted spin turns flat, the engine will stop. With two of us in the airplane, the only way to force the nose down to initiate a recovery is for me to climb into the front seat with you." I smiled at the mental image of me squeezing over Kennedy's shoulder wearing a parachute while the airplane was whipping around upside down. I think he had not considered that the carburetted engine in the Citabria would quit when held inverted.

Kennedy looked at his watch and cut my briefing short. "Well, we have just enough time for a short flight. I have to be somewhere else this afternoon."

"Yes, sir," I replied.

I signed the flight sheet and followed the unhappy man out the door. When I reached the Citabria, I said, "I completed the pre-flight inspection before you arrived but I'll do another one if you'd like."

"No, that won't be necessary."

He climbed into the front seat.

"While you're belting in," I said, "I'll brief you on the emergency procedures."

"That won't be necessary either," he grunted.

"Well, if we have a structural failure," I said timidly, "I need you to jettison the door and jump out so I can follow."

As he finished buckling the seat belts, he said, "We are not going to do anything to cause a structural failure. I have no intention of exiting this aircraft in flight."

"Well, sir," I said less timidly, "if you don't go, I can't go."

"Young man, I have survived many problems in the air, including a Chipmunk on fire, without jumping and I'm not going to start now."

"Have it your way," I replied. "If you don't mind, let me show you how to release the door so I can jump."

To myself, I said, And so the rescuers will find you in the wreckage with my footprints on your back.

"Very well," he replied.

I showed him how to pull the pins on the door hinges and then climbed into the rear seat.

"As the front seat student, you'll have to start the engine for us and set up the radio communications," I said as I buckled my harness. "The checklist is in the pocket ahead of your right knee."

Kennedy didn't bother to reply but he dug out the checklist and began running through it. When he reached "engine start," he barked, "All clear!" out the door, then closed it and pushed the starter button.

Kennedy ignored me while he finished the post-start checks, turned on the radio and picked up the microphone.

"Circus Ground, this is Citabria Lima Oscar Oscar Papa, ready to taxi for a local flight to the west."

"Lima Oscar Oscar Papa, ground, Runway 24, wind calm, altimeter 29.98, taxi Charlie Bravo."

"Lima Oscar Oscar Papa."

Kennedy added power and taxied toward the runway. "I assume you can fly from the back seat," he announced, "so I'll get us going."

"Yes, sir, help yourself," I replied.

He parked beside the runway and completed the pre-take-off checks.

"Circus Tower, Lima Oscar Oscar Papa, ready for takeoff, straight out departure requested," he said into the mic.

"Oscar Oscar Papa, you are cleared for takeoff. The wind remains calm. Straight out departure is approved."

"Oscar Oscar Papa."

Kennedy applied power, moved onto the runway centreline and then took off.

We climbed to the practice area without talking. When we reached 4,500 feet Kennedy told the tower we were clear of the control zone.

"Cleared on route, Oscar Oscar Papa."

"Oscar Oscar Papa," he replied and then hung up the mic.

"Assume that I have had the initial ground briefings on a loop, roll and spin," Kennedy called over his shoulder. "Demonstrate those three manoeuvres to me. You have control." With that, he held both hands up to indicate he was not flying anymore.

"I have control," I responded.

I talked my way through the safety checks. Kennedy just looked down at the scenery without commenting. When I came to the beginning of the loop, he tightened his belts and then reached for the V-shaped struts running from the instrument panel to the top of the windshield. He held onto them with both hands.

I pushed the control stick forward to build up speed. I had never practised aerobatics with the weight of a passenger. I added extra speed and pulled back harder. The result was a gut-wrenching, egg-shaped loop but we made it all the way around.

I leaned forward and declared, "Student practice sir. You have control."

"That won't be necessary," he grunted. "Carry on."

I demonstrated a barrel roll to the left. The Citabria was no Chipmunk when it came to control response and I was no Ben Ivory but we rolled fairly well. Kennedy continued to hang onto the windshield struts.

"And now for the spin demonstration," I announced.

"I'm ready," Kennedy said.

I described what I was doing as I pulled the airplane's nose up and booted it into a spin to the right. The Citabria obliged by flicking into a tight, nose down rotation. I let it wind up through several rotations.

"Recover!" Kennedy barked.

I obliged.

As I was pulling out of the dive, Kennedy said, "Take us back to the airport."

He didn't say whether I had passed or failed but it was clear that the flight test was over.

"Would you like to fly on the way back, sir?" I offered.

He looked around outside and then released his grip on the windshield

struts. "All right," he said, "I have control."

"You have control, sir," I replied. "The airport is straight ahead."

"I know that."

As Kennedy set up a descent toward the airport, I caught movement out our right side. I turned to see a familiar Chipmunk easing into formation under our right wing.

"Looks like we have company at four o'clock low," I said to Kennedy.

He looked to the right and gave a little start as the Chipmunk pulled in tight. I could see Ben Ivory in his flight suit looking at us with a big grin. He waved his face mask at us to indicate radio contact.

"It's Colonel Ivory, sir. I think he wants to talk on the air-to-air frequency."

"I can see that," Kennedy answered impatiently.

He switched the frequency on the radio and picked up the microphone. "This is Lima Osar Oscar Papa, to the Chipmunk, go ahead."

"Doomer, how you doing?" Ben's voice boomed back. "This is your old instructor Colonel Ivory. How are you making out with my student there?"

"We are fine, colonel," Kennedy said nervously. It was obvious from his voice that he was uncomfortable having Ben flying so close or talking so informally, or both.

"We are heading back to the airport, so please stand off," Kennedy announced. "I'm switching over to Circus Tower now."

"Roger, dodger Doomer," Ben replied. "I'm headed for the barn too. You've got the lead. I'll follow."

"Lima Oscar Oscar Papa, out."

Ben eased his airplane an extra wing-span away and stayed with us. Kennedy kept looking ahead and then to the right like he was trying to fly both airplanes. He called Circus Tower and announced that he was approaching the airport control zone for a landing. The controller responded with instructions to join a right-hand downwind leg for Runway 24.

As soon as Kennedy had acknowledged the transmission, Ben's voice came on the radio.

"Circus Tower, this is Foxtrot Lima India Papa also returning for a landing. I have the numbers. I'm following the Citabria and have it in sight."

"Lima India Papa, Circus Tower, roger. Follow that traffic for the right-hand downwind to Runway 24."

"India Papa."

While these transmissions were taking place, Ben had been descending slightly faster than Kennedy. The Chipmunk was dropping lower in the formation. Kennedy pushed his stick forward and reduced the power so he could keep the other aircraft in sight. Soon both airplanes were in steep, power-off descents.

Just before we reached 1,000 feet above ground, the altitude where we would be leveling off to approach the runway, Ben eased the Chipmunk up in the formation. The change created a strong optical illusion in the

Citabria. It felt like we were suddenly dropping faster. Kennedy instinctively pulled back on the control stick. The Chipmunk continued to rise relative to us making it look like we were still falling.

"What the...!" Kennedy exclaimed. He pulled harder on the stick. The Chipmunk was now well above our wing. With that, the stall horn sounded. Kennedy and I both looked ahead. We were in a nose up attitude with no power. Kennedy dropped the nose and applied full throttle. The Citabria staggered for a second and then flew out of the stall. The Chipmunk was no longer in sight.

"Oscar Oscar Papa, Circus Tower, I see you're joining the right downwind for Runway 24. You look a little low, are you experiencing any difficulty?"

Kennedy fumbled for the microphone, "Oscar Oscar Papa," he replied. "No problem here but we've lost sight of the Chipmunk."

"The Chipmunk is well behind you, Oscar Papa," the controller assured him. "You're cleared to land."

"Oscar Papa."

"Lima India Papa, Circus Tower, you're number two to the Citabria. Do you still have the traffic in sight?"

"Affirmative, India Papa."

I could hear the smile in his voice.

Chapter Eleven

The Big Apple

Any misgivings I had about hiring Leanne Rains when we started The Flying Circus had been dispelled on her first day. My partner's wife took immediate charge of the office. She applied ten years of motherhood to effectively overcome any lack of business experience and aviation knowledge. Leanne's handling of a call for a charter flight was a good example.

I returned from a flying lesson. After my student left, Leanne announced, "I booked you to fly a greenhouse salesman to Planehaven, New York for a one o'clock meeting tomorrow."

"Leanne, I have students tomorrow."

"Not anymore," she replied. "You had two. I juggled things around. Henry and Barry can fly them. You'll be leaving at eight o'clock in the morning."

I went to the map on the wall. I had never heard of Planehaven. As I warmed up to the idea of going somewhere new, I hoped it would be further than the 50-mile hops around the lake to Toronto.

"Where is Planehaven?" I asked, looking past Niagara Falls.

Leanne walked to the map. She reached up and stabbed the middle of Long Island, New York with her finger.

"I measured 320 nautical miles," she declared. "I figured three hours flying in a Cherokee, plus a half-hour stop for customs."

"Wow! That's our biggest flight yet!"

I took the plotting string and stretched it from Circus to the Planehaven Airport. Leanne was right, it was 320 miles away. I'd be gone all day, maybe two. Business was looking up.

Then I saw that the route ran through a huge yellow area on the map near the destination. It was New York City, the world's largest metropolis and the busiest airspace. I had never flown there. I didn't know if you were allowed to in a small airplane, and if you were, whether you would want to.

"Leanne, that's New York City on the route."

"Yes, I saw that," she answered cheerfully. "The Big Apple; you'll see all those tall buildings, the Statue of Liberty and Times Square. It has to be the most exciting place on earth."

"It's the excitement I'm worried about."

Leanne ignored me. "Imagine all those people," she continued. "You never know, maybe you'll meet somebody famous!"

"Not likely," I replied. I looked on the chart for routings around New York's major airports. "I'll stay as far away from the big city air traffic as possible. I'll be looking for other aircraft, not celebrities."

At that point, Henry walked through the door. He saw us looking at the map on the wall.

"Another charter?" he asked expectantly.

"Yes!" Leanne exclaimed. "To Long Island, New York."

"Hey, that's a good one!"

"Yeah, but you'll have to fly through New York City's airspace to get there," I added. I wanted to see his reaction if he thought it was his flight.

Henry joined us at the map. He followed my finger across New York City. "I see what you mean. When is the trip?"

"Departing first thing tomorrow," I replied.

"Well, you've got lots of traffic experience around Toronto," Henry suggested, "and I had the last long charter. Why don't you take this trip and I'll fly your students?" He looked at Leanne.

"It's already arranged," she replied. "Mr. Big City Charter here departs at eight o'clock in the morning."

"Oh, good. You should be fine. Just avoid the middle," he advised. He circled a finger around the tight maze of control zones created by La Guardia, Kennedy and Newark airports. "Use the radio and keep your head up."

I sighed in agreement.

Henry slapped my shoulder. "You do the flight planning and I'll get an airplane ready for you."

Leanne held out her hand. "Here's the company credit card for gas and ten dollars American money that I always carry in my purse."

"What can I buy in New York for ten dollars?" I asked.

"Nothing I hope. The cash is a loan for emergencies but I want it back. Give my regards to Broadway."

At 7:45 the next morning, I was checking over the Cherokee on the ramp. A small car zipped into our parking lot. The driver's door popped open and a man jumped out. He grabbed a briefcase and a long, fat tube from the rear seat and hustled toward me.

"I'm Peter van der Root," he announced as he trotted closer. "Are we ready to go?"

I introduced myself and said, "Yes sir, can I help you with your things?"

"It isn't necessary," he answered curtly. He jogged past me to the side of the airplane.

Van der Root was medium height, lean and in his forties. He's body language was all, "go, go."

"I'll ride in the back," he declared. "I have work to do on the way."

"Ah, the back seat is kind of small," I answered.

He looked in the side window. "Can you remove that seat?" he asked, pointing to the front passenger seat.

"Ah, yes, I suppose I could," I answered slowly. I wasn't an aircraft mechanic but I decided that removing a seat couldn't be difficult. "It'll take a few minutes. Would you like to wait in the office?"

"How long?"

"Ten minutes."

"I'll wait here."

It took me five minutes to find the tools and another five to fit the right size wrench to the bolts that prevented the seat from sliding off the front of its track. Van der Root shifted impatiently from one foot to the other and checked his watch frequently. I was having trouble undoing the first bolt. It was tight against the floor and I was upside down.

"Let me have a look," van der Root suddenly said. It was more of a command than a question.

I straightened up and saw that he had dumped his case and tube on the ramp and was ready to climb onto the wing.

"I can see how it should be done," he explained briskly.

He was the one in the hurry so I didn't argue. I climbed down and held out my handful of tools.

Van der Root ignored the offering, hopped onto the wing, leaned in and moved the seat full forward. Then he reached down behind it and pulled out two clips from the rear of the tracks. This allowed him to roll the seat all the way back and lift it up. He eased it out the door.

"Here," he said, holding the chair out for me. The look on his face was neutral and there was no malice in his voice.

"Thank you," I replied lamely.

I nearly dropped the whole thing. The little man had handed it to me like it was light. It wasn't.

As I turned toward the hangar, van der Root reached out and stuffed the two clips into my shirt pocket, saying, "Don't lose these."

I nodded and waddled off with my load.

I stashed the seat, clips and tools in the hangar. I returned to find van der Root already sitting in the airplane. I hopped onto the right wing. The inside of the 140 looked roomier with the seat gone but van der Root was quickly filling the extra space with blueprints that he was pulling out of the tube.

"Ready to go?" I asked.

"Yes, yes," he said quickly.

I stepped in and swung over to the pilot seat. As I was closing the door, I launched into a passenger briefing. Van der Root spread a blueprint on his lap and ignored me.

"Is your seat belt fastened?" I called out.

"Yes!" he answered sharply.

I started the engine and called the controller for instructions. There was no other traffic. I taxied out, completed the checks and took off.

We were headed for Scranton, Pennsylvania first. I planned to clear into the United States with American customs there. The stop would also give us a stretch and a bathroom break. I mentioned this to van der Root.

"Whatever," he replied without looking up.

The weather was a bit hazy but otherwise clear. We flew over Niagara Falls, Buffalo and the hills of western New York State. The leaves on the trees were starting to show their fall colours. Van der Root saw none of it. He stayed buried in his blueprints.

"Coffee?" I asked, holding up Henry's old thermos and a cup.

"No thank you," he replied smartly. "I don't drink coffee."

It was his longest sentence of the morning. I helped myself.

I was beginning to like this charter flying. It generated more money per hour than the flying lessons, was easier on the airplane and I didn't have to teach. I just applied what I knew to flying and navigating.

As I cruised along, I wondered why airline pilots needed so much help to complete a similar trip. They had a cockpit full of big-dollar navigation equipment, an autopilot, a copilot, air traffic controllers with radar and the backing of the whole airline infrastructure. I guessed they were paid more than flying instructors because they had to learn to use that stuff.

The Cherokee flew southeast into Pennsylvania. This was new territory for me. I divided my attention between map reading and enjoying the scenery. The smooth early-morning air gave way to light turbulence as the sun warmed the ground and the hills grew higher. The haze thickened and the visibility dropped. I did less sightseeing and more navigating.

Scranton is a good-sized city that shares an airport with nearby Wilkes-Barre in Pennsylvania's industrial heartland. For the last 50 miles of that leg, I followed the Susquehanna River Valley which the map indicated would lead to the Scranton Airport before it veered southwest. I did a groundspeed check. We were making good time.

As we neared Scranton, the mountains steepened and the haze turned to smog. I was having trouble matching zigs and zags in the river to the ones on the map. I flew on. I tuned the airplane's only radio navigation aid to the Wilkes-Barre VOR. It showed that I was on track but the transmitter was not located right at the airport. I did not have any electronic distance information.

I was determined to impress my passenger as well as the air traffic control system with my professionalism. I selected the frequency listed for Scranton's automatic airport information. I listened to the short recording twice around and noted that 22 was the active runway. The airport visibility was given as six miles but looking into the sun, it seemed much less.

I set up a descent from 3,500 feet and selected the Wilkes-Barre Scranton Tower frequency. I estimated I was about 10 miles outside the airport's five-mile control zone. There was no talking on the receiver.

I summoned a deep, airline-type voice and pressed the microphone transmit button. "Wilkes-Barre/Scranton Tower, this is Cherokee Charlie Lima Alpha November Delta."

"Cherokee calling Wilkes-Barre, squawk 2271 and call Wilkes-Barre Approach on one two four point five."

"Alpha November Delta."

There was nothing on my visual flying chart to indicate I should have called an approach controller. So much for sounding professional. I selected the squawk code he gave me on my transponder. This would identify me on their radar. I changed communication frequencies as requested and ditched the low voice.

"Wilkes-Barre Approach, this is Cherokee Charlie Lima Alpha November Delta."

"Charlie Lima Alpha November Delta, Wilkes-Barre," the controller answered calmly, "radar contact four miles northwest of the Wilkes-Barre Airport; say your altitude and heading."

According to him, I was already in the airport control zone. The tailwind must have pushed us further than my inaccurate map reading recognized. I felt my face turn red.

"Descending through two thousand, five hundred," I replied, "and heading one seven zero."

The river was below but I couldn't see an airport ahead.

"On that heading, you'll miss the field," the controller said. "Turn left to zero four zero, radar vectors for a right downwind to Runway 22. Stop descending until you have the airport in sight."

"Left turn to zero four zero," I answered timidly. "I'm leveling at twenty-two hundred feet."

"US Express 111, you're number one for Runway 22 four miles back, contact the tower now on one two zero point one."

"Two zero one, roger, Triple One," a deep voice replied.

I did not have a headset so I was listening to the radio over the cabin speaker. I hoped van der Root was too engrossed in his plans to follow my amateur transmissions.

I leaned forward to see better over the nose. In front of me, the city was spread up both sides of the valley but there was no sign of an airport.

"Alpha November Delta, you are number two for Runway 22 following a Jetstream on short final. The airport is at your two o'clock position for two miles. Advise when you have it in sight."

I looked to my right. I could see buildings, roads and railroads below but no airport. "Negative contact," I replied.

"The airport just went under the wing," van der Root announced from the back seat.

I banked right to drop the wing and there it was. I had been looking in the valley but the airport had been carved out of the ridge, part-way up. I could see the runway and the Jetstream turboprop approaching the end.

I pressed the microphone button, "Runway in sight, November Delta."

"Roger, Alpha November Delta, you are cleared to descend and are number one on the approach; contact the tower now one two zero one."

"Alpha November Delta."

I reduced the power, pushed the nose down and turned to make sure I didn't lose sight of the runway. The tower controller cleared us to land.

I could hear van der Root rolling up his blueprints. I landed and was directed to the customs ramp at the end of the terminal building. Despite our little detour we were ahead of schedule.

By the time I had shut down the airplane, van der Root had stashed his paperwork under my seat and was sitting calmly with his arms folded. A U.S. Customs agent walked toward the airplane. He was tall and lean. His dark uniform, badge and sidearm made him look like a sheriff. I opened the door on the right side.

"Good morning," I said with exaggerated cheerfulness. I didn't have much experience crossing the border but I had heard bad stories from other pilots.

"Good morning," the officer replied as he walked around the right wingtip. He wasn't smiling but he wasn't frowning either. He leaned in the door opening while still standing on the ground. "Citizens of what country?" he asked. He was looking at me.

"Canada," I replied.

He looked at van der Root.

"Canada."

I handed him the immigration form that I had filled in on the way.

"What's the nature of your business in the United States?" he asked

Van der Root interrupted, "It's a business trip."

while skimming over the form.

"It's a..." I started to say.

Van der Root interrupted, "Business, it's a business trip. We are going to see greenhouses on Long Island."

"How long will you be in the United States?" the agent asked.

"Returning to Canada later today," the salesman replied.

"Are you carrying anything that you will be leaving in the U.S.?"

"No sir," van der Root said.

"Have a good day." He turned and walked toward the terminal.

"I spoke up," van der Root explained, "because I have experience crossing the border as a Canadian businessman."

"That's fine with me but what's the problem with allowing a Canadian businessman into the United States?"

"If I had said that I'm on a sales trip to Long Island to sell Canadian-made greenhouse equipment that beats everything they have here he would have been unhappy. Instead, I said that I was going to see greenhouses on Long Island. His question was answered and it was the truth. He went away happy."

"Oh."

"Ready to go?" van der Root asked.

I was except for my need to vent the coffee I had consumed.

"Do you want to use the washroom?" I asked hopefully.

"No, no, let's keep going," he replied looking at his watch. "We must be there before one o'clock."

"OK, we're off."

I closed the door and started the engine. Van der Root pulled out his blueprints and spread them open.

There was no traffic. We were cleared to taxi and take off without delay. Climbing in the haze, I picked out the highway that I knew would lead me north of New York City.

There were so many airports packed into the New York area that the markings on the map for their various control zones created a confusing kaleidoscope of interlocking circles.

To avoid as many zones as possible, I planned to fly north of the main airports and then turn southeast after crossing the Hudson River. This would require flying over five miles of ocean to reach Long Island but it looked like the path of least control zone resistance.

I leveled off at 3,500 feet. When we were outside the Wilkes-Barre radar area, the controller cleared me on route and gave me a New York Centre frequency for radar following. I switched to it. A fast-talking controller with a nasal New York accent was peppering instructions to several aircraft in one continuous transmission. It was optional for me to contact him so I listened to hear if I could get a word in.

"United, turn left radar vectors to zero five zero, cleared to nine thousand; American, over to New York on 122.275 now; Air Canada, keep the speed up, cleared to five thousand, contact 122.275..."

I had never heard a controller operating without replies. I had been taught to read back radar instructions to confirm that I had received and understood them. This guy talked for five minutes and not one pilot responded. When he finally paused for a moment, nobody jumped in.

I decided the busy controller didn't need to hear from a visual flying Cherokee pilot at low level. I turned down the volume and watched for other aircraft. The sun was off to my right now and I could see six to eight miles. I was able to follow our position on the map. As we flew closer to New York, I descended to 2,000 feet to stay underneath the outer ring of the mandatory contact area. Closer in, I would have to talk to someone or fly east to Connecticut and cross a wider section of the Atlantic Ocean to get to Long Island. I didn't want to cross that much water at low altitude in a small plane.

I selected the close-in New York frequency to listen ahead. The controller was using the same unbroken, rapid-fire technique as the previous one. Occasionally he asked a quick question and received a snap reply from a pilot but there were no pauses where I could jump in.

I could see the Hudson River ahead. At that moment the controller told another aircraft to watch for unidentified eastbound traffic west of the Hudson with no altitude readout.

"Contact," the pilot replied. "It's a small fixed-wing at two thousand."

I spotted a large helicopter going the other way passing below and to my right.

"Thank you, over to Teterboro now nineteen five; Hudson Shuttle, right to one seven five, vectors around traffic..."

I realized that they must have been talking about me. I held the microphone to my lips and jumped in at the next pause.

"New York, Cherokee Charlie Lima Alpha November Delta, crossing the Hudson at two thousand eastbound to Planehaven."

"Cherokee to Planehaven, squawk 1163; Hudson Shuttle, left to 155; seven Uniform Papa, over to Teterboro now nineteen five; six Papa Golf, right to one seven zero, down to three thousand; Cherokee November Delta, you can't go that way, turn right to two zero five and descend to one thousand five hundred, don't acknowledge; 33 Delta, cleared..."

I turned and pointed the Cherokee's nose down.

I knew that van der Root would not approve of a detour but we were committed.

"Six Papa Golf, over to Teterboro now on nineteen five; Cherokee November Delta, click once if you're level one point five."

I punched the mic button.

"Good, you are on radar vectors along the Hudson until south of JFK, switch to one two seven six and wait for a call; niner X-Ray Hotel, cleared to three thousand, left to one seven zero..."

I changed frequencies. We were flying along the narrowing Hudson River. The skyscrapers of downtown Manhattan emerged from the haze a few miles ahead.

"...seventy-seven Hotel, over to tower now eighteen seven; Alpha November Delta, right to two one five; one two Tango Tango, right one six five..."

I became aware that van der Root had stopped rustling his blueprints

and was leaning forward to look ahead.

"Nice view of New York, eh?" I offered.

"The controller just told you to turn right to two one five degrees," he replied calmly.

"Are you sure?"

"Positive."

The turn was only ten degrees so I did it knowing it wouldn't make much difference.

The closer we came to the downtown core, the higher the buildings appeared. The tops of several looked like they would be above us. Two large helicopters crossed our path, one above and one below.

"...Shuttle forty-four, change to PanAm pad; November Delta descend to one thousand, change to New York now one twenty-eight fifty-five; ninety-nine Mike Bravo..."

I nodded to van der Root to show I had heard, set up a descent and switched frequencies. I didn't know if I should call this controller but I didn't have to wait long to find out.

"...Delta, you're on the centreline, over to tower eighteen three; Canadian Cherokee you should be at one thousand, watch for traffic below that I'm not talking to; Northwest, cleared..."

I leveled off at 1,000 feet. We flew along the middle of the river beside the downtown. There were buildings above us. It felt like we were in a manmade canyon with vertical walls of glass, steel and concrete. Not turning ten degrees would have been a mistake. I looked down.

The river was busy with ferries, tugs and barges. Times Square was on the left and the Statue of Liberty stood guard just beyond. The suspension towers for the bridges spanning the Hudson seemed to reach up trying to touch our airplane.

"Ellis Island is on my side," van der Root said. He sounded almost excited. "That was my grandparents first stop in North America."

"Cherokee November Delta, change New York, one twenty-seven four; Shuttle fifty-five, over to..."

I switched frequencies and heard, "...ember Delta, turn ten degrees left; American, radar contact, turn right to..."

I picked up my microphone to confirm the controller had been talking to me but there was no chance of breaking into his transmissions.

I turned hoping that I was right. The river began to widen and we were leaving the tallest buildings behind. On my left, I could see airliners climbing from the JFK Airport.

"...Alpha November Delta, left to one seven zero; Northwest, radar contact, right to..."

It looked like we were being steered gradually around the south side of Long Island underneath JFK's departing traffic.

It looked like we had landed in a 1950s' aviation zone.

"...November Delta, change to JFK twenty-five twenty-five; Lufthansa, radar contact, through two thousand, turn left..."

I rotated the frequency selectors again.

"...two two; Alpha November Delta, left to one three zero; United, contact..."

A few minutes later, we were given another turn that headed us east. I could see parallel runways at JFK pointed at us less than ten miles away. Later we were allowed to climb to 1,500 feet.

I was told to change frequencies four more times before the controller said, "...November Delta, Planehaven is on your left, heading zero two zero, six miles, squawk twelve hundred, cleared on route; nine three Papa, turn to..."

I wanted to thank him for the help but he continued to talk to other aircraft. I turned to 020 degrees and switched the radio to Planehaven. There was no control tower there but a unicom frequency was assigned to the airport so pilots could announce their location to other traffic.

There was no one talking on the frequency. I picked up my microphone and announced that I was five miles away inbound for a landing. No one replied.

The visibility was reduced in haze. I realized that I had better map read to find the airport. There were no radar vectors here and we had left the seashore behind. I stared at the ground ahead willing the airport to appear.

Van der Root tapped me on the shoulder. "It's on my side," he announced, pointing down.

I circled to the left until I could see Planehaven's two paved runways forming an "L" shape. It looked like a friendly-sized airport tucked into the side of the City of Planehaven.

I flew overhead and decided the windsock favoured Runway 24. I announced my intentions and turned to a left downwind leg for a landing.

I could not see or hear other air traffic. I landed and taxied to the apron. There was little sign of activity. It looked like we had landed in a 1950s' time zone. Several old Navions and Swifts were tied down in the grass with a Seabee and a triple-tailed Bellanca. There were a couple of similar vintage hangars and a small terminal building. The only shiny aircraft was a Beechcraft Baron parked with its door open in front of the terminal. I stopped beside the fuel cabinet nearby. The time was 12:50.

Two men came out of the terminal and walked our way. Van der Root climbed out and onto the wing carrying his tube and briefcase. He waved to the men, hopped to the ground and started toward them. As an afterthought, he turned and said, "I will be three or four hours."

"That's fine," I called back but he was already greeting his customers. They shook hands, walked around the building, climbed into a car and drove off. I breathed a sigh of relief.

Chapter Twelve

Runaway Diner

I sat in the cockpit for a few minutes on the Planehaven ramp trying to relax. My heart was still racing from the high-pressure radio work. As the gyro instruments wound down, so did my tension. It was replaced by increased bladder pressure. I climbed out of the airplane and walked the short distance to the terminal building. Inside, the sagging wooden structure looked and smelled like an old, small-town railroad station. The bare walls were covered with multiple layers of cracked, smoke-stained, green paint. The floor tiles that weren't missing were well worn. There was no one in sight.

I used the closet-sized washroom and then looked around. A grubby handwritten cardboard sign on the roadside door read, "Back at 1:30."

I stuck my head outside. There was a car parked in front of a long, narrow, cinderblock building not far up the road. I headed that way.

As I walked closer, I could see that the flat roof was covered with old wavy plywood. A faded sign above the screen door read, "Runway Diner."

The backside of the building was facing the airport. The solid wall had a strange pattern in it that resembled the rough shape of an airplane. It stood out because the blocks and mortar were a different colour of gray. There was the shadow of a third shade of blocks outlining it. I opened the door under the sign and walked in.

It was a classic diner like thousands scattered along America's secondary highways. On the ceiling, painted particle-board sagged between strapping. It was accented with water stains and hanging strips of curled flypaper.

Two older men were sitting on the middle stools of a tiny lunch counter facing the road. They both turned and gave me a polite, "Hello."

I returned the greetings.

On the left, small tables with empty chrome chairs were placed along the wall where the same airplane outlines appeared in the blocks.

If Clouds Could Talk

Another man emerged from a small kitchen beyond the counter. He was wiping a white platter. The dish contrasted with his food-stained apron and T-shirt. With a stubble beard, round belly and mostly toothless smile, he looked like Wimpy, the hamburger man in the Popeye cartoons. He nodded in my direction and ducked back into the kitchen.

I took a seat at the counter. The two men went back to eating their lunches. I looked at the letterboard menu on the wall. It had been there for a while. Missing characters had left their outline as clean spots on the plastic background.

The grill man came back out of the kitchen wiping his hands on the dirty apron. "Da special is a dozen steamed clams in butter for tree-fifty but I make udder stuff," he offered with a smile. His squeaky voice sounded friendly but it didn't match his large size.

The thought of 12 slippery clams before a bumpy flight home didn't sit well. I looked at my neighbours' plates. They were eating chicken sandwiches.

"I'll have what they're having," I replied.

"Comin' right up," the cook squeaked.

The man sitting beside me turned and asked, "Where're you from?"

He sounded pleasant but he was a little rough looking. His clothes were rumpled and he was wearing a hairpiece that a dog must have used as a toy.

"Canada," I replied.

"Big country," he mused. "Any particular part?" His deep voice whistled through a missing front tooth.

"Yes, sorry; Circus, near Niagara Falls."

He and his buddy nodded knowingly.

"You just landed a few minutes ago, did you?" he asked.

"That was me."

"Well, welcome to the famous Run-a-way Diner at Planehaven International Airport," he said offering a handshake. "I'm Cliff and this is Bob."

I introduced myself, shook Cliff's hand and nodded to Bob.

The cook stepped out of the kitchen with a chicken sandwich on a platter flanked by a few potato chips and half a pickle.

"Wanna drink?" he squeaked while sliding the plate in front of me.

"Water will be fine."

My counter mate nodded toward the cook. "This is Daisy, the chief cook, bottle washer and owner of the Run-a-way Diner."

"It's da 'Runway Diner'," Daisy corrected, "except to some of my unwashed regular clientele. And since when did da airport become 'international'?"

"Five minutes ago," Cliff answered, "when our Canadian friend here landed."

Daisy smiled. "You came to da right diner but you sat wit da wrong crowd. Just pay no mind to dese guys."

Cliff and Bob grinned.

"Thanks for the warning," I said.

"Don't listen to him," Cliff countered. "His mother wanted a girl and we think she got one."

I ate some sandwich and then asked Cliff, "Is there a story behind the Runaway Diner nickname?"

Bob smiled; Cliff pointed to the outline on the wall behind us. "The locals call it 'Abbey's Backstop.' Abbey is Abigail Duncan, Dr. Duncan's wife. She took flying lessons in the Doc's Beech Musketeer. The instructor sent her on a first solo on Runway 24. She took off all right but came in high and fast for the landing. Instead of going around, she tried to stop. The airplane skidded off the runway, across the grass and into the diner."

"Wow. That sounds like a bad one."

"Well, no one was hurt," he chuckled. "The tables were empty and the airplane stopped halfway to the kitchen."

Daisy came out carrying my water. His eyes were bulging. "I t'ought da freight train was comin' t'rough. Dat crazy woman opened da door of dat plane and started yellin' about my diner bein' in her way." His voice squeaked higher when he was excited.

"Did she leave you a tip?" Cliff asked with a laugh.

"She never pay nuttin'," Daisy exclaimed.

"That explains the airplane pattern of newer blocks," I said.

"Partly," Cliff continued. "After her first, first solo, the diner wall was rebuilt and the Doc bought a Bonanza. A few months later, the same instructor sent Abbey up for a second first solo on the same runway. On that landing, the airplane didn't penetrate as far."

"Dat's because I put garbage cans full of sand along da wall," Daisy smiled.

"What are you doing for next time?" Cliff asked.

Daisy's grin dropped. "She don't fly no more, right?"

"Well I don't know," Cliff said nudging Bob. "I heard the Doc was looking for a Baron."

"If dat's true, den I'm out of here," Daisy declared.

"You said that the first time," Bob chuckled.

I joined the fun. "Daisy, maybe you could install one of those service station bells that ring when a car drives over the cable. Then you'll know when she's coming."

Cliff and Bob laughed.

"Dat's just what dis diner needs," Daisy said, shaking his head, "anudder joker." He smiled and walked back into the kitchen.

"Are you guys with the Baron parked outside?" I asked Cliff.

He nodded and Bob spoke, "Cliff just bought it and I'm checking him out."

"Great looking airplane," I enthused.

"Thanks, it is," Cliff replied and then grinned. "Bob's an FAA flight inspector and he's here to help me."

They had obviously known each other for a while. I ate more of my lunch and then said, "Bob, may I ask you about flying through New York City from here?"

"Sure, it's not hard. You can pick up your clearance by radio here on the ground. Then you call ATC when airborne. The controllers do the rest."

"I'm flying VFR."

"Ooh, that's a little tougher. Fly low and go the long way around the control area to the north," he suggested. "Just don't go anywhere near the main airports or Manhattan. How did you get here?"

I could feel my face blushing. "I contacted ATC and flew radar vectors."

"Did they give you the big detour into Connecticut?"

"No, quite the opposite. I was vectored straight down the middle of the Hudson River and then along the south shore of Long Island."

Both pilots looked at each other in surprise. "You were steered over downtown New York?" Bob asked.

"More through it than over it," I replied. "At one point they had me down to one thousand feet."

"That's unusual," Bob exclaimed.

"I guess I won't try that way going back."

"You're better off filing IFR," Bob replied.

"The Canadian government doesn't allow IFR charter flights in single-engine aircraft."

"They think VFR at one thousand feet over Manhattan is safer?" Cliff asked.

"Well, we don't have any Manhattans in Canada and I don't have enough equipment in the airplane to file IFR," I replied.

"Tell you what," Bob interjected. "We're just about ready to go. Come out to the Baron with us and I'll give you a New York ATC number to phone and ask for the best VFR routing."

"That would be great, thanks."

"By the way," Bob added with a big grin, "have you figured out who Cliff is yet?"

"I'm sorry, I don't know anyone in Long Island," I replied.

Cliff smiled.

Bob continued. "Since he told you I work for the FAA, I'll tell you that he's Cliff Robertson, the actor. You know, PT-109, Charlie, and stuff like that."

"Oh sure. I'm sorry I didn't recognize you," I said to Cliff.

"That's OK. I'm in disguise."

"Disguise, my foot," Bob said. "He always looks like this. For the movies, it's the Hollywood make-up artists who make him look good."

Cliff grinned again. "Ready to go partner?"

We paid for our lunches. "Good to meet ya," Daisy said to me and then lifted his head toward the others. "And if you two are goin' to fly touch and goes on dis runway, I'm closin' up."

"You'd better start filling those garbage cans with cement," Cliff laughed.

I followed them to the Baron. Bob started a walkaround inspection and Cliff climbed onto the wing and reached into a flight bag behind the front seat.

"Come on up and have a look, if you like," he offered. He pulled out a book and stepped back. "Have a seat and I'll look up the number."

"Thank you."

The airplane shone inside and out. I sat in the right front seat and drank in the rich smell of the new leather. The instrument panel was loaded with dual dials and radios.

"The seats in this airplane are worth more than my Cherokee," I said enviously.

Robertson tore a page from the book. "I learned to fly in an airplane like yours," he replied. "The extra power and equipment I got with this bird just gets me into trouble faster." He handed me the page. "I circled the phone number that Bob mentioned."

"Thank you very much."

I took the page and hoisted myself out of the seat. When I was standing beside the actor, I hesitated and then said, "Would you mind autographing this for Leanne, the receptionist back home?"

"Not at all," he crooned in his deep voice. He took the page, scribbled on it and gave it back to me.

"Give her my best," he whistled through his missing tooth.

"Thank you, I will."

I jumped down from the wing as Bob walked around the Baron's tail.

"Thanks for the help," I said to him, waving the piece of paper.

"You're welcome," he replied with a smile. "Good luck."

"Thank you, I hope I don't need it."

Chapter Thirteen

Lessons from Long Island

As the Baron was climbing out from the runway, a pickup truck pulled into the terminal building parking lot. I was standing beside the Cherokee. A short, round, middle-aged man climbed down from the driver's seat and looked my way. He was dressed in the green work shirt and pants of a municipal employee.

I waved. He started walking to the terminal building but changed his mind and ambled toward me.

"You don't want fuel do ya?" he called out from a distance. He sounded hopeful that I would say, "No."

"Yes sir, I do."

"How much?" He continued to walk slowly in my direction.

"I need both sides filled."

"Well, I hafta turn the pumps on inside," he grumbled loudly. "I don't wanna find out you're down just a couple of gallons." He stopped within talking distance of me.

I gave him a smile and replied, "No sir, I wouldn't do that to you."

"Ya know," he continued, "besides runnin' the airport and pumpin' fuel, I'm also the airport gardener, landlord, plow driver, janitor and security guard. In fact, I'm the only city worker at the airport."

"Well sir, I'm glad you're here," I replied.

He grunted and waddled off to the terminal building.

When he returned, I listened to him complain for a few more minutes. As long as he was talking, he wasn't fueling so I excused myself and took a map over to the pay phone outside the terminal.

I called the number that Cliff Robertson had given me. The person answering spoke like a New York Air Traffic Controller, quickly and with attitude. "New York Centre."

I spoke as fast as I could. "I'm a pilot in Planehaven and I'm calling for the best route to fly VFR from here toward Scranton, Pennsylvania."

"Fly north 40 miles; stay below 3,000 and then turn left. Don't call any New York IFR frequencies."

"Do you want me to call anyone else?"

The line was dead. He had hung up.

I looked at the map. Van der Root and I were going to see part of the Atlantic Ocean, a piece of Connecticut and lots of New York State on our departure. I sat on a bench beside the phone and plotted a course north and then west over to my inbound route.

I walked back to the airplane. The gas man was reeling the hose into the cabinet.

"I'll hafta figure this out inside," he said.

I knew he wanted to talk more than "figure" so I let him go ahead. I tossed my map into the Cherokee, checked the fuel levels and then pushed the airplane back so it was not blocking the pumps. Then I went into the terminal.

The airport guy was sitting scratching his head in a tiny office near the front door. "It comes to thirty-eight sixty," he announced.

I pulled out my company credit card and handed it to him.

He looked at it from an arm's length. "I've never seen a card like this," he grunted.

"It's Canadian," I offered.

"I can't take foreign money here. Don't you have cash, American?"

"It's an international card that was issued in Canada. It'll work here and you'll receive American dollars."

"Easy for you to say," he countered, handing back my card. "And I get stuck with the bill when it doesn't. Give me an American card or real American dollars."

"I don't have either," I replied.

"Then you're not going anywhere until you do." He stuck out his chin to emphasize that he meant it.

"When my passenger returns, I'm leaving," I declared just as stubbornly. "If you won't accept the card, then pump out the fuel or give me a bill and I'll send you the money."

"Hey, Mack, this is Long Island," he said, shoving his jaw out further. "In God We Trust; everyone else pays cash. The pumps don't pump out; I don't accept foreign cards; and you don't fly anywhere with my truck chained to your airplane's nosewheel."

This guy is as stubborn as he is thick, I thought to myself. I considered explaining how the card worked internationally or asking him to phone a local bank. I didn't do either. It was three o'clock. Leanne would be leaving The Flying Circus office. If I needed her help, it had to be now.

"I'll phone my office and see what I can do," I said.

"American cash," he replied. "The pay phone's outside."

I went out and called The Flying Circus. Leanne answered.

"How's Broadway?" she asked.

"I'm stuck off-Broadway with a fuel man who won't take our credit card. Can we arrange for you to wire some money or something?"

"Oh, I was just going home."

"Well, I'm stuck here unless we can come up with a way to pay in American dollars."

"Is he there?"

"He's not far away."

"Let me talk to him."

I had no idea what Leanne planned to say to the guy but her voice was in "take charge" mode so I didn't question her.

"Give me a minute," I replied.

I rested the receiver on top of the phone, stepped out of the booth and leaned through the front door of the terminal.

"My office manager wants to speak to you," I called out.

The airport man hoisted himself out of his creaky chair, shuffled around his desk and headed my way.

I held the front door open. He gave me a dirty look as he passed.

"American cash," he muttered.

He went into the booth and picked up the phone. "Hello?"

I leaned against the glass and listened.

"Well, this pilot says all he's got is a foreign card. I can't take it.

"Yes ma'am.

"I understand but I don't have a fancy machine that tells me if it's good or not.

"Yes ma'am.

"But I could get into trouble.

"Yes ma'am.

"Yes ma'am.

"Yes ma'am."

His expression changed from defiance to submission.

"Yes ma'am.

"Whatever you say, ma'am.

"Yes ma'am.

"Yes, I will."

He hung up and shuffled past me back into the building. I followed. He sat down at his desk and heaved a big sigh.

"Give me that card again," he said holding out his hand.

I gave it to him.

"What did she say?" I asked.

He took the card wearily. "She said the card would work," he moaned. "I could take it or be in more trouble than I had ever known. Along the way she mentioned my mother, an international incident, congress, the president, my pension, me hanging from a cross and World War III. Who is she anyway?"

"My boss."

"If you work for her," he said, jerking his head toward the phone booth, "you have my sympathy."

"Thank you."

We finished the transaction. I went out to the Cherokee. The car carrying van der Root returned a few minutes later. The greenhouse salesman climbed out of the back seat smiling. He shook hands with his customers and walked quickly toward the airplane.

"Ready to go?" he asked in his clipped voice.

"Yes sir," I replied. I motioned for him to climb in. "After you."

It was a long trip home but van der Root didn't seem to mind. Once we were airborne, he chatted away cheerfully about the scenery, flying, greenhouses and Long Island. It turned out that he had made a big sale. He was very happy.

I flew the detour to the north, as requested. When we turned west, it was a slow ride into the wind. Van der Root eventually opened his briefcase and did some work.

We flew home non-stop. It took four hours. The sun was setting when a Canada Customs officer met us at the Circus Airport main ramp. Van der Root did the talking and we were cleared in.

I taxied over to The Flying Circus. Henry was waiting for me. Van der Root thanked us for the flight and hustled off to his car.

"Well, how did it go?" Henry asked.

"Fine," I replied, mimicking his minimal responses. The difference was that Henry would let the question drop. I'd have to keep talking if I wanted him to know.

"Our passenger made a big sale and is very happy. Hopefully we'll get more business from him."

"Good. How did the airplane run."

"Fine."

"OK, let's go home."

The next morning when Leanne came in, I was on the ground between lessons.

"Hey, thanks for the help with my fuel bill yesterday. You were a life saver."

"You're welcome," she smiled. "The guy wasn't as stubborn as my own kids."

"What did you say to him?"

Leanne blushed and then spoke in a voice that I had never heard before. She sounded like she had eaten glass and gravel for breakfast.

"It's what ya say and how youse say it," she snarled. "When ya wanna play da game, youse gotta speak da language. I insulted his ancestry and then threatened him with an international incident."

"Wow, that's impressive. What other languages do you speak?"

"The same as every other mother," she replied.

"Well thanks again."

She smiled. "I guess you didn't see much of the Big Apple. Henry explained that you'd have to go around the city because of the busy airports and would be landing on the other side of it. It's too bad you didn't get to fly over the downtown."

"Actually, I did see downtown Manhattan."

"You mean from a distance?"

"No, we flew right down the middle of the Hudson River below the tops of the tall buildings. We saw the traffic jammed in the streets, the river and the Statue of Liberty."

"Sure, next you'll tell me about the famous people you met."

"Just one. After we landed, I had lunch with Cliff Robertson, the actor."

"Oh sure," she laughed, "and my name is Katherine Hepburn!"

"Seriously," I said, pulling the signed page out of my pocket, "I got his autograph for you." I handed her the sheet.

She looked at it. "Cute trick," she replied, handing it back. "You scribble Cliff Robertson's name on scrap paper and expect me to fall for it. My kids could teach you better fast ones than that."

"No, really," I protested. "Cliff was at the airport lunch counter when I arrived. He had landed to take a break from being checked-out in his new airplane. We sat next to each other."

Before Leanne could say any more, the telephone rang. She reached for it.

"I'll get it, Mister Celebrity Hunter.

"Good morning, The Flying Circus.

"Yes, he's right here."

"It's for you," she said. Then she placed her hand over the mouthpiece and gave me a huge, fake grin. "It sounds like Cliff Robertson."

I took the phone. "Hello?"

"Hi, this is Cliff," a familiar voice said. "We met yesterday at Daisy's restaurant on Long Island."

"Yes, Cliff. I remember. Thanks for your help."

"You're welcome. Bob and I were a little concerned about you flying around New York VFR so I told him I'd call and see how you made out."

"Thank you, Cliff," I said loudly. Now it was my turn to flash a cheesy grin at Leanne. "I didn't have any problem. Bob was right. New York Terminal didn't want me near them so I took that big tour to the north."

"Well, I'm glad it worked out. Maybe we'll meet at Daisy's again."

"I'd like that."

"Bye for now."

"Ah... before you go, would you mind speaking to our receptionist again and tell her who's calling?"

"Not at all; put her on."

I held out the phone to Leanne. I couldn't believe my luck. "Cliff Robertson wants to say, 'Hello.'"

Leanne's expression was turning from tough mom to little girl. She took the phone.

"Hello?"

She listened for half a minute. Her eyes grew wider.

"Thank you sir... I mean Mr. Robertson. I will. Bye, bye."

She hung up the phone, thought for a moment and then reached over and grabbed the autograph from my hand.

"Who was that, Leanne?" I asked in a singsong voice.

"He said it was Cliff Robertson."

"Well, wasn't that nice of him to call?"

Leanne didn't hear me. She stared into the distance and swooned. "He asked me to keep the autograph handy in case he needed one of the phone numbers. If he did, he said that he would call back."

Then she looked at me. "I apologize for accusing you of pulling a fast one." She was clutching the paper to her dress.

I smiled. "How do you know I didn't?"

Chapter Fourteen

"Yes I can!"

The office door flew open and Summer McDay bounded in. "Good morning," the young blonde sang cheerfully.

"Hi there," I replied. "What brings you to the airport today?"

"I came to see you about aerobatics," she announced with a big grin.

Summer was the bright and bubbly sister of Instructor/Controller Barry McDay. She was studying sports medicine at the local university. She also worked part time at The Flying Circus some evenings and Saturdays, trading receptionist duties for flying lessons.

"Aerobatics usually come after the pilot licence, Summer. What's your rush?"

"I'm bored with the basic course. I'll probably never finish it. I thought I'd try aerobatics just for fun."

I wasn't surprised. This was a girl who had taken up skydiving as a high school credit but I didn't respond to her right away. I suspected that Summer would have trouble flying aerobatics in the Citabria. The seats in it were not adjustable. Neither were the rudder pedals. The airplane was built to be flown by average-sized males and Summer was, at the most, five feet tall.

I looked at her clear blue eyes. They were waiting for a reply but I knew that I'd be in trouble if I suggested to this sparky young lady that she was too short to fly aerobatics.

"Well, Summer," I said slowly, "let's go to the hangar and you can try the airplane on for size."

"All right!" she whooped.

I grabbed an armload of cushions from the lounge and followed her out the door.

The Citabria was the first airplane inside the hangar. I opened the right-side door with one hand while holding the cushions with the other.

"Climb into the front seat, Summer," I said, "and see how it fits."

"Lift yourself up for a second," I said.

She hopped onto the step and into the cockpit with athletic ease. Once she was seated, I said, "Try looking out the windows."

Summer had to stretch to see over the side windowsill. She had no forward view at all in the nose-high airplane.

"Lift yourself up for a second," I said, "and sit on this pillow."

I shoved the largest cushion under her. This helped her see out the windows but her feet were a long way from the rudder pedals.

"Shift forward and see if you can reached the pedals. I'll stuff pillows behind your back."

She wiggled ahead. I slid first one, then two, then three cushions behind her. Now she was perched on the edge of the seat and the control stick was wedged firmly against the part of her anatomy that was at the top of her legs. Her feet were still not touching the pedals.

"Gee, Summer," I said in mock surprise, "it looks like you won't be able to fly this airplane. You can't reach the rudder pedals."

She looked down at the stick and the pedals. Then she pivoted her body around the stick clockwise and stretched her left foot forward far enough to stab the left rudder pedal. Next she twisted around to the right until she could reach the right pedal. She gave it a shove and then looked at me.

"Yes I can!"

"Well, Summer," I smiled, "you need to move the control stick too. Aerobatics in this airplane call for full deflection of the ailerons."

She looked at the stick, gripped it in her right hand, lifted her left leg high and pushed the stick underneath. Then she moved it back to the middle, changed hands, lifted her right leg and pushed the stick full deflection to the right. She centered the stick, dropped her leg and turned to me.

"See!"

"OK, Smarty," I laughed, "but how will you work the elevators up and down?"

Summer turned in the seat 90 degrees and lifted her left leg onto the seat. With her back to me, she leaned her body out of the way, and pulled the stick to full-up elevator. Then she moved toward the instrument panel and pushed the stick forward.

She peered at me over her right shoulder. "See!"

I admired her resourcefulness but I could not imagine her actually flying the airplane that way. "I don't think so, Summer. It's one thing to improvise on the ground but you can't do aerobatics like that."

The blue eyes flashed defiantly. "Yes I can!" she insisted.

"You'll be wasting your money and my time," I replied.

"Do you want to bet? What are the manoeuvres in the first lesson?"

"A loop, hammerhead and roll."

"If I can do all three, the lesson is free. If I can't do any one of them, I'll work double time to pay for it and I won't bug you again."

It was apparent that I would have to fly with Summer to show her that she couldn't fly the Citabria.

"OK, if you're so game, we'll go back to the office for a briefing."

"Yahoo!" she yelped. She hopped down from the cushions and led me out of the hangar.

I briefed the young athlete on flying the Citabria and described how to do the first three aerobatic manoeuvres. She asked the right questions and seemed to understand my answers.

We went back to the hangar and completed the pre-flight inspection together. Then Summer helped me push the Citabria out to the ramp. She climbed onto the cushions in the front seat. I helped her fasten the wide aerobatic lap and shoulder belts. Then I climbed into the back.

The instructor sat in the Citabria bobsled style with his feet on either side of the front seat. I had a control stick, a throttle and rudder pedals. Everything else was up front including the starter, communications radio and instruments.

I buckled up and looked forward. Summer was so short; I had my best view ever from the rear seat.

"Go ahead when you're ready, Summer," I said.

The gutsy girl followed the checklist. She had to hunt around for some of the switches but she managed to start the engine without much trouble. Then she called the ground controller and was given instructions to the active runway.

The taxiway headed off to the right. Summer pivoted around the control stick until she could stab the right rudder. The airplane started turning. To stop the turn, she slid around and pushed the left rudder. We wandered our way to the runway as Summer wiggled from pedal to pedal. It must have looked like the pilot was drunk but the controller didn't say anything about it to us.

Summer completed the pre-take-off checks and then called out, "Are you ready to go?"

"Affirmative," I replied.

She radioed the control tower and was cleared to take off.

Handling a tailwheel airplane on departure was different from what we taught in the Cherokees. I had covered this during our briefing but just in case she was nervous, I asked, "Do you want me to do the takeoff?"

She didn't reply. Instead, Summer steered the Citabria onto the runway, shifted around in her seat and stretched her right leg forward. She held the stick back with her right hand and applied full power with her left.

The Citabria accelerated. Summer moved the stick forward and jabbed some right rudder to correct a swing to the left. The tail came up and we headed down the runway more or less straight. At flying speed, she eased back on the stick and we were airborne.

As we climbed out, she turned and grinned, "No thank you."

I had to smile. "OK, Supergirl, try a few shallow turns during the climb."

Summer banked in and out of turns in both directions. She flew the airplane well for a first timer, especially considering that she had to contort like a circus performer to reach the controls. Her success meant that we had to do aerobatics to prove that she was too short to fly a Citabria.

I had briefed Summer that we'd start with a loop and had explained how to fly one. Loops are one of the easier aerobatic manoeuvres but are more difficult than they look. The engine in the Citabria was rated at a maximum 108 horsepower when it was new. It was not powerful enough to pull the airplane through a loop from level flight so we always started with a shallow dive to build speed. Then the nose was pulled up sharply and full power added. The pitch-up caused the aircraft to yaw left as it did on takeoff. Pressure on the stick was varied as the airspeed dropped. Approaching inverted, the back pressure and rudder were relaxed at the lower speed to keep the loop more or less round. Ailerons were used to keep the wings level. As the airplane's nose headed toward the ground, the power was reduced to idle and the stick pulled harder as the speed built up again. Power was reapplied and the stick neutralized in level flight.

"When you're ready," I said, "do a cockpit check, look around for other traffic and try a loop."

"OK," she sang out.

Summer completed the safety checks and then pivoted around the stick until her back was against the door. She was anticipating the need to pull the stick all the way and to push right rudder. She eased the nose down. When the speed approached 120 mph, I shouted, "Go for it!"

She hauled back on the stick with her right hand and leaned forward to apply full power with her left. The nose headed skyward and yawed left. Summer stabbed the right rudder. We continued pitching up but the speed dropped quickly. The airplane was approaching straight up when its forward momentum died completely. Another part of Summer's anatomy had prevented her from pulling the control stick all the way back.

I had never been in a tailslide before.

In the Pilot Operating Handbook for the Citabria there was a list of aerobatic manoeuvres that were prohibited. "Tailslide" topped the list.

The airplane slid backward but not for long. The nose plunged forward into one almighty whipstall and then pendulumed back and forth a couple of times before settling into a nearly vertical dive.

"I have control!" I yelled.

Summer turned toward me. "No you don't!" she declared.

She was right. I had a hand on my stick but it wouldn't move. Summer had firm control. She reduced the power and pulled up elevator. We were pressed into our seats as the airplane swooped out of the dive. Summer pointed the nose skyward, using the extra speed to regain some height. Then she reapplied power.

"Nice try, Summer, but I guess you can't fly aerobatics in this thing,"

I yelled above the engine noise. "Do you want to head back to the airport now?"

She didn't answer. With no further acknowledgement of my existence, the determined little pilot leveled off from the climb and checked around for traffic. I was along for the ride, for better or worse.

Summer reached under the back of her sweatshirt, unhooked her bra and pulled it out from underneath. Without looking, she tossed it into the back seat. It landed in my lap.

She turned counterclockwise in her seat and pushed forward on the stick. When our speed hit 120 mph, she two-handed the stick back past her more mobile chest. The nose shot up. Summer applied full power and stabbed the right rudder. I was pressed into my seat again as the Citabria arched up and over the top of a loop. As we flew onto the backside of the manoeuvre, Summer pulled the throttle back. The airplane continued pitching around to level flight. She moved the stick to neutral and turned in my direction.

"Yes I can!" she declared.

This meant that we had to do the next manoeuvre to prove that she couldn't fly aerobatics.

"OK, try the hammerhead," I said. "You might not be able to reach all the controls to do one properly."

Summer looked for traffic and then pivoted around the control stick clockwise until she was looking out the door-side window. She knew from our briefing that full left rudder was needed to skid the airplane around.

A hammerhead turn is a reversing manoeuvre that starts with the first part of a loop followed with a skidding rudder turn that takes the airplane from straight up to straight down. It finishes with a dive recovery.

When she was ready, Summer pitched the nose forward to gain speed and pulled the stick with both hands past her chest. The throttle was under her left armpit so to add power, she lifted her left elbow, crossed her right hand underneath and pushed the throttle lever all the way forward.

The Citabria zoomed skyward but it started yawing to the left. Summer reacted quickly by stretching her left leg across the cockpit and stabbing the right rudder pedal which straightened out the nose.

When we were approaching vertical, she moved her left foot over and applied full left rudder. The airplane skidded left but she had forgotten that it would also roll left as the accelerating right wing gained lift. The Citabria rolled onto its back, the nose dropped and we plunged into a spiral dive. The speed increased rapidly.

"May I have control now?" I questioned loudly.

"No!" the feisty coed replied. She reduced the power to idle, leveled the wings and pulled out of the dive.

"I guess the hammerhead is harder than a loop," I said. "There's no sense knocking yourself out. Are we returning to the airport now?"

Summer didn't answer. She completed the safety checks, turned in her seat 90 degrees to the right and lifted her right leg into the air. She commenced a dive, leaned back and hauled on the stick. Her right hand shot under her left arm to add power while her left leg crossed over to push the right rudder pedal.

As we approached straight up, Summer changed rudder pedals and pushed the left one all the way. Then she added full right aileron to prevent the roll by moving the stick under her right leg. She looked like she was in a strange yoga position but she didn't forget anything and her timing was excellent.

The Citabria skidded around in a nice flat hammerhead. When we were pointed straight down, she neutralized the ailerons with the stick, crossed her left foot over to the right pedal to centre the rudder, reduced the power to idle with her right hand under her left arm and pulled out of the dive.

The airplane pitched up to level flight. Summer turned toward me and said, "See!"

"Well, done," I replied, "but the roll is next and it's more complicated. Shall we skip it?"

"No."

We had briefed on a barrel roll to the left. Summer did her safety checks and then turned in her seat until she was facing left. She lifted her left leg and pushed the stick forward to build up speed. At 120 mph, she brought the nose up to the horizon, applied full power and then shoved the control stick under her left leg. The Citabria started rolling to the left but the drag of the right aileron caused the nose to yaw right. Summer counteracted by extending her right foot across to the left rudder and pushing it.

As the airplane rolled inverted, Summer ran into trouble. Neither one of us had noticed that her gyrations around the cockpit had loosened her seat belts. When the Citabria went upside down, Summer slid out of her harness and fell onto the cockpit ceiling with a thump. She held onto the stick. Her weight pulled the controls to the middle. The airplane stopped rolling. We were flying inverted. The Citabria's engine was not equipped to run upside down, so it quit. Now we were gliding inverted.

I looked up at Summer and said tentatively, "May I have control now?"

She didn't answer but she let go of the stick. I shoved it to the left. There was enough momentum remaining in the glide to roll us right side up. As the airplane came around, gravity dropped Summer unceremoniously onto her seat. She bounced onto the floor.

I leaned forward and called to the pile of Summer that was gathering herself up. "I guess we found a manoeuvre you can't do."

She didn't reply. I continued to fly. I eased the Citabria into a turn toward the airport.

My stubborn student picked herself off the floor, sorted out her seat belts, sat down, put them on and snugged them up. Then she grabbed her control stick and wiggled it. It was obviously the signal that I was no longer in control.

Summer looked around for traffic and then entered a shallow dive. When we had picked up speed, she raised the nose to the horizon. Without turning in her seat, Summer lifted her left leg up and shoved the stick under it. The Citabria rolled left. The nose yawed right. Summer reached down with her left hand and grabbed my left shoe on my left rudder pedal. She pushed it, applying hard left rudder. The airplane obediently rolled over. Passing through inverted, she moved the stick forward to keep the nose up while holding aileron and my shoe for rudder. As we approached right side up, she neutralized the aileron with the stick and centred the rudder by pulling my shoe back.

She turned her head and said, "Yes I can!"

"OK, you win," I declared, shaking my head. "The lesson is free. Now can we go back to the airport?"

"Sure," she replied. "Hang on!"

Summer turned the Citabria toward Circus by rolling it over in that direction. Then she pulled loops all the way to the control zone.

On the ground, she climbed out of the Citabria grinning from ear to ear. "How about going double or nothing on lesson Number 2?" she asked.

"Not a chance," I replied.

"I'll book it anyway," she laughed.

Chapter Fifteen

Cargo master

Olaf Petterson called. A bulldozer on the road-building job north of Sudbury had broken down. An equipment dealer in Derry, not far from Circus, had the needed part.

"Can you take the Citabria to Derry, pick up the part at the airport and fly it to the job?" he asked.

Leanne was running errands in town and Henry was flying with a student. I pulled out the charter book that my efficient partner had prepared for such a request. Under "cargo" was a list of questions.

"When did you want to book the flight, Mr. Petterson?"

He sighed impatiently. "Now," he said.

"How much does the part weigh?" I asked.

"I don't know," Petterson replied. His voice carried an edge that indicated his tolerance for fools was being tested.

I continued down the list. "What are its exterior dimensions?"

"Look," he said, it sounded like his teeth were clenched, "the part is bigger than a breadbox and a lot heavier. It's a steering knuckle. I don't know the exact weight but I flew in that airplane and I know the part's not as big or as fat as me. Can you take it or not?"

I abandoned the charter manual and checked the booking sheets. Henry was scheduled to give lessons most of the afternoon but I had only one student.

"Yes," I replied.

"Then you'll have to get moving to beat sunset. The part will be waiting at the Derry Airport."

"I'll leave shortly."

"Good. Call me before you depart Derry northbound."

"Yes sir."

He hung up.

"Good-bye, sir."

I checked the weather and phoned Barry. He was working the morning shift in the control tower but said that he could instruct my student.

I was gassing up the Citabria when Henry taxied in from a lesson. I told him about the trip. He briefed me on how to find the straightened piece of road at the job site and marked it on my map.

"You shouldn't have any trouble getting there," he offered, "but you'll have to hustle. You don't want to be flying back over the bush in the dark."

I hadn't thought about the return. "OK, thanks."

"And take some rope so you can tie down the cargo," he added.

"Will do."

"Have a good trip."

I finished fueling and grabbed some rope from the hangar. I jumped into the airplane and was about to start the engine when Henry trotted out of the office waving the coffee thermos. I opened my door.

"It's just water but you'll need something."

"Great." I waved my thanks and stowed the thermos under the front seat. I started up and looked at my watch. It was two o'clock. It would be dark around seven. The flight from Derry to the job would take about three hours. I would run out of daylight on the way home but not until I'd flown over the worst of the bush.

The weather was good but the flight to Derry was into a strong wind. It took 30 minutes. The Derry Tower Controller directed me to the approach. I had to follow two training airplanes that were flying wide circuits. I landed, taxied to the ramp and shut down near the terminal building. A bright yellow pickup truck was parked on the other side of the chain-link fence. A burly driver stood next to it.

I hopped out and waved to him. "I'll be with you in a minute," I yelled.

He nodded.

I jogged into the terminal building and headed for the security office. The door was open. I could see an elderly guard sitting with his feet on a desk. His eyes were closed. He looked frail enough that his next scare could be his last.

"Excuse me," I whispered from outside the door.

He didn't move a muscle.

"Hi there," I said louder.

No response.

"Under the B, fourteen!" I announced.

He woke up with a start.

"Hi," I grinned. "I just arrived in an aircraft and I need to have the gate

"What is the aircraft registration?" he asked slowly.

opened to allow a truck onto the ramp to transfer some cargo."

The guard rubbed his face, lifted his feet off the desk and leaned forward. He plucked a stubby pencil from behind his ear, licked the point and set his hand onto a daily log sheet.

"What is the aircraft registration?" he asked slowly.

"L-O-O-P," I replied.

He wrote an "L" in the first space in the log and then stopped.

"It doesn't start with 'C'?" he asked.

"Yes, it does. C-L-O-O-P."

He turned the stub over and rubbed the eraser over the wet "L" on the page. It smeared. He looked at me like it was my fault.

He started on the next line. "C-L...," he said aloud and then stopped.

"O-O-P," I offered.

He finished the entry.

"Who owns the aircraft?" he asked.

"It's registered to The Flying Circus," I replied.

He slowly printed, "the fliing sircas." I didn't try to correct him.

"Address?"

I gave him the information. The clock on the wall read 2:45.

"What kind of aircraft is it?"

"A Champion Citabria," I replied.

The guard pulled out a booklet, adjusted his glasses and started thumbing through it.

I was getting antsy over the time. "What are you looking for?" I asked loudly.

He slowly looked up from his reading. "The weight of the airplane."

"Under two thousand pounds," I replied.

He wrote that on his log-in sheet.

"That will be twenty-five dollars," he said.

"Twenty-five dollars!" I exclaimed. "For what?"

"Landing fee."

"I've landed here before and never paid a fee," I protested.

"Give me the dates," he replied, pencil in hand, "and you can pay them all now."

At this point, I realized that the guard wasn't sleepy any more and I might be arriving up north in the dark.

"Look," I said leaning forward, "it's a fabric-covered, two-seat airplane. There should be no landing fee. Now I'm in a rush. Will you please open the gate?"

"It's a commercial flight. The charge is twenty-five dollars."

"That doesn't make sense. I have flown here to pick up a part from one of your tax-paying local businesses. You want me to pay a landing fee?"

"Yes."

"If I flew here for fun and did business with no one, would it be free?"

"That's right. If you don't have the money, we can bill you," he offered.

I didn't have time to argue. "Fine, bill me. Now can we open the gate?"

"Right away, sonny."

It took five minutes for the old guard to shuffle outside to the gate. Another five minutes was lost while he sorted through a large ring choked with keys. He opened the gate and the trucker drove to the airplane.

I should have removed the rear seat. Petterson was right; the part was in a box smaller and lighter than he was but not by much. It took two of us to carry it to the airplane. After much struggling, grunting and a few bad words, we had it standing on end in the back seat with the other end pressed against the ceiling. The rear control stick hit the box when I pulled it back. The truck driver had some tools that I used to remove the rear stick. I thanked him and checked my watch. It was 3:30. If nothing else slowed me down, I would be arriving over the job site at sunset.

Then I remembered the rope in the baggage compartment. I couldn't reach it without unloading the cargo so I secured the four-point aerobatic harness around the box. Now the cargo looked like a real passenger. If I had not been in a hurry, I could have drawn a face on the box and talked to it on the way.

As I climbed into the front seat, I realized that I was supposed to call Petterson before departing Derry. I jumped back out and hotfooted into the terminal building. The first thing I saw inside was the security guard shuffling along on his rounds.

"Hi, is there a pay phone?" I asked.

He looked up and took his time focusing on me but didn't say anything.

I raised my voice, "Is there a pay phone in here?"

"Yes," he replied, continuing to stare at me.

"Where?" I boomed.

He lifted an arm and pointed to a phone on the wall less than 20 feet

I removed the rear control stick. The cargo looked like a real passenger.

away.

"Thanks!"

I called Petterson's office. His secretary said he was on another line. That was fine with me. I didn't have time to explain why I was so late departing Derry. I left a message and headed back outside.

I looked at my watch as I climbed into the Citabria again. The time was 3:45. I punched the starter and was already moving when I called for taxi instructions.

I departed, turned north and leveled off at 2,000 feet. I set the throttle at maximum cruise rpm to get the best speed and then leaned the mixture control for the best power. The needle on the airspeed indicator settled on 103 mph. I was getting an extra five-mph at the cost of seven American gallons per hour instead of six. The 35 gallons that I had when departing Circus would give me five hours before fuel exhaustion. As I cleared the Derry Control Zone, I had burned nearly an hour.

The rushing around on the ground had made me anxious, sweaty and thirsty. I guzzled some water from the thermos and tried to settle down.

I stayed at 2,000 feet until I had passed the Toronto area and then climbed to 6,500 feet where the air was thinner. In level flight with full throttle, I calculated my true airspeed at 110 mph. I was hoping to get a little tailwind on this leg but it was the end of the day and the wind was dying. I timed my distance over two points on the map. The groundspeed worked out to 105. If I could maintain that, I should be over the job site by 6:15; enough time.

I started to relax a little. I had rarely flown without a passenger or a student. It was nice to fly along and enjoy the view but it was cold at that altitude. My lightweight fall jacket was not warm enough. I pulled the heater knob to "on." It didn't work. As I shivered, I realized a pressing need to pee. I hadn't been to a washroom since lunchtime back in the office.

I ignored my bladder's call as I flew to the bottom end of Georgian Bay on Lake Huron. From there, I followed the 30,000 islands scattered along its eastern shoreline north toward Sudbury.

I passed the time by justifying a return flight at night. I listed the trouble created by staying over. I would need to call my neighbours to feed my dog at the house. Someone else would have to fly with my students in the morning. If no one was available, they would be cancelled and we'd lose the revenue. Where would I stay at the construction site, what would I eat and how would I keep from freezing to death? What would the weather be like tomorrow?

To fly back that night, I just needed to arrange for fuel in Sudbury and then keep going. The weather was good. I could fly high and glide if I had an engine problem.

It was getting colder. I really needed a pee stop. I thought if I was ahead of my estimated time, I could land at Sudbury on the way up, refuel the airplane and de-fuel my body. Then I could fly home non-stop from the construction site. I checked the groundspeed. It was 96 mph, not good. The light wind must be slightly on my nose. I'd have to keep going.

I flew over the Sudbury Airport at six o'clock. I radioed the fuel man who said he would be there until nine p.m. Perfect.

I had 70 miles to go but the sun was touching the horizon. It was autumn and the daylight hours were getting shorter.

Henry had shown me on my map how to follow a line of hydro towers that crossed the road under construction.

"Follow them and turn right at the road. You can't miss it," he had said.

I found the row of towers. In the failing light, the hydro right-of-way looked like a giant razor had cut a straight swath through the solid bush. There were not many other landmarks. I had to concentrate hard to keep track of my progress. My only distractions were the cold and my bladder.

I felt like I was going to wet myself. It would not look good for the pilot to arrive with smelly, wet pants. Then I remembered the thermos. I asked myself if I would dare use it. My answer was that I could clean it out later and no one would know. I hauled it out and drank the rest of the water. Then I removed the seat belts and unzipped my fly. There wasn't much to work with when the cold air hit my bare skin. It was a juggling act to hold the thermos, pee and fly the airplane at the same time. Luckily the air was calm but I was still making a mess.

Next I realized that the thermos was filling up and I didn't know how to stop in mid-stream. I finished off by filling the cap from the thermos. Now I had two full containers. I placed them gently on the floor on either side of the control stick. They danced from the engine vibration.

I opened the window on the left side. It was hinged at the top. An arm stopped it from opening more than six inches. I picked up the cup and slowly tipped it toward the opening behind me while enduring a frigid air stream in the side of my head. Most of the contents splashed down the inside of the airplane. The rest spread itself along the outside. I decided not to try the same thing with the thermos. I closed the window, stoppered the thermos and replaced the cap. Now I had to find the power lines again.

The sun had set but there was some light left in the sky. I looked ahead and saw the power lines off to the right. Further ahead I also saw an oasis of bright lights on the ground. I thought it must be a lumber mill in operation. I looked on the map. There was nothing there except the "X" that Henry had marked as the landing strip location. Then I realized that the construction guys must be working under the lights. It was 6:30.

I eased the Citabria's nose down with the control stick and headed for the glow. I kept the power on to gain speed in the descent.

The lights were so clear that they seemed to be close but it was another 20 minutes before I was turning over top of them. Looking down, I saw two rows of construction equipment, one parked along each side of the straight piece of road. Their lights were shining on the runway. Portable light stands marked each end.

I turned on my red and green wingtip lights and the landing light in the Citabria's nose. I circled to the east, did a pre-landing check, slowed down and lined up with the twin rows of lights about a mile away. Ahead the glow from the sunset remained in the western sky. Below was darkened bush.

I wiggled in my seat and sat up to spike my concentration. It was the end of a long flight and the landing was not going to be easy. Twilight was harder to land in than daylight or darkness. I nailed 70 mph on the airspeed indicator and descended toward the narrow strip.

The landing area was supposed to be over 2,000 feet long and 70 feet wide. From half a mile back, it appeared more like inches than feet. The near end was approaching quickly. I aimed to just clear the light standard. I was too high and the airplane was drifting to the left. I rolled the right wing down and pushed left rudder for an exaggerated sideslip. The height came off and the airplane realigned with the strip. I could now make out the headlights on individual pieces of equipment. The road still looked impossibly small and was approaching fast. For a second I thought of trusting that everything would work out. It would look professional to drop the airplane into the strip on the first try but my backside felt like it was being dangled over a buzz saw.

"What are you doing?" I asked myself out load.

This was not what I taught my students when arriving over a strange, questionable landing strip. I applied full power and initiated an overshoot.

The go-around gave me a chance to look closely at the landing area. I flew its length with the right wing down. It seemed big enough from this close overhead. I could see workmen looking up at me. Some waved their hard hats. I pulled the nose up and circled to the right.

The wind at ground level was calm which explained why the approach seemed too fast. I lined up for a landing again. This time I was lower so I wouldn't need as much sideslip. I resisted the temptation to slow below 70 mph. The airplane would lose enough speed transitioning into the calm air.

I wiggled and stretched once more. This should be it, I thought.

Approaching the first lights, I checked my airspeed. It read 65 mph. Close enough. I pulled the throttle back to idle. As I sailed over the light standard, I was lined up with the middle but there was very little room between the rows of headlights. I eased the nose up. Now the airplane was committed to land.

The Citabria dropped onto the road with a plop. My speed had been a tad low. The airplane vibrated as it skated on the washboard pattern left by the bulldozers. I danced on the rudder pedals to stay straight and eased on the brakes.

I stopped before the far end. I added power to make it to the turn-around. I could feel my body tingling from an adrenaline rush. I swung the airplane around, ready to depart the other way after unloading.

As soon as I had shut down, a pickup truck stopped beside me. A short, stocky guy hopped out and trotted over to my door. I opened it. He looked surprised for a moment.

"Hi, I'm Rocky the foreman," he said, "but you're not Henry."

"Right, I'm his partner."

I introduced myself.

"Pleased to meet you," Rocky replied. "Thanks for coming."

"Happy to oblige."

I went to undo my seat belts and found them dangling on the floor. I hadn't refastened them since relieving myself.

I turned in my seat and released the belts from around the box. "It'll take two of us to wrestle this thing out of here," I said.

"No problem," Rocky replied. He leaned into the back seat, slid his beefy arms around the box and started wiggling it.

"If you let me out, I'll give you a hand."

"It's OK," he grunted. "I got it."

With one more tug, he pulled the container off the seat and out the door. It must have been half his height and nearly his weight but he didn't drop it as he staggered over to the truck. I climbed out and followed him. Then I realized that the equipment operators were shutting down their headlights.

"Rocky, I was planning to take off for home right away. Can we get those lights back on for a couple of minutes?"

The foreman dropped the box into the back of the pickup.

"I talked to Olaf and he said you were staying. I guess he talked to your partner."

"Well, I've worked it out so I can still make it home with a stop in Sudbury for fuel, but I'll need the lights to depart."

"Why not stay?" he countered as he slammed the tailgate closed. "You can have dinner at the lodge with the boys while I help the mechanics get started on installing this knuckle. There is lots of food. It's off-season for the lodge."

"I'd rather head home now," I pleaded. "I have flights tomorrow morning."

Rocky walked toward the truck cab. "Olaf said your lessons tomorrow will be covered by some part-time guy. He said you could fly some of us over the job in the morning, after the weather clears up. Then fly home in daylight." He opened the driver's door and started to climb in.

"If the weather is going to turn bad," I replied loudly, "I'd like to go now. I don't want to get stuck here!"

The burly man stopped and thought for a moment. Then he got out of the truck and stepped close to me.

"Look," he said quietly but clearly, "we just met but I run this job. We thought you would have arrived two hours ago. We could have repaired the dozer in daylight before supper. But you didn't..."

"I... I..."

I was about to explain why I was late but Rocky held up a hand.

"It's OK," he continued. He kept his tone even but strong. "We worked while we waited. When the sun set, we lined up the equipment so you'd have lights if you were still coming. You found us and did a nice landing. Now I'm going to take the knuckle over to the dozer and get the maintenance guys started on it."

While he spoke, I could see some of the workers approaching in the pickup's headlights. Rocky leaned closer and lowered his voice.

"The way I see it, you've got two choices. You can yell and scream like a prima donna pilot or you can relax and be one of the boys for the night. These guys have been on the job since seven this morning. They're overdue for a hot meal but I don't hear them complaining. You're welcome to join them at the lodge or you can go hungry and sleep out here tonight. What's it gonna be?"

As Rocky was giving me his straight talk, my adrenaline drained quickly. He was right. I was pushing too hard. It wouldn't hurt me to stay and it would be a lot smarter than flying back in the dark. Besides, it appeared that taking off was no longer an option.

"You're right, Rocky. I'm sorry. I'd be happy to stay."

"Good man." He smiled and slapped me on the shoulder. Then he turned toward the truck. As he climbed into the driver's seat, he pointed to the men. "These guys will help you secure the plane and give you a ride to the lodge." Then he lowered his voice and smiled. "You'd better zip up your fly. It's been a long summer. You don't want to look like you're trolling for action with this bunch."

Chapter Sixteen

Stinky

I secured the Citabria with help from some of the men. One of them pointed to a crew-cab pickup truck not far away. "That's your ride," he shouted.

I walked over and opened the rear door. Two burly equipment operators were already filling most of the back seat.

"Climb in," the nearest one said, shifting against his buddy. "We don't want to keep the cook waiting any longer."

There were two other workers in the front seat.

"Oh, lordy no," the guy on the passenger side of the front seat echoed. "We're in trouble already."

I squeezed in. It took two tries and more shifting before I could close the door.

"I'm Wendel," the driver said without turning around. He put the truck in gear. "This here's Jed," he added pointing to the man beside him. Wendel floored the accelerator as Jed nodded. Both men were as big as the back-seaters. "And you're sittin' with the Hardly twins."

I introduced myself. "I appreciate the lift."

"Jed was happy to see ya come in," the twin beside me said with a chuckle. "It's his machine that's broke."

"Ya, we're glad to see you too," the other twin added. "Jed's been on the survey pole since he broke down and we're goin' crooked for sure." He laughed. Jed turned and smiled. They all seemed in an end-of-day happy mood.

"Do you guys have first names?" I asked the twins.

"Orville and Wilbur," Wendel called from the front seat as he sped through the construction.

"They can't tell us apart," the guy next to me said. "So they call both of us 'Hardly'."

"You guys can't tell yourselves apart," Wendel replied.

The other twin leaned forward. "The name's actually 'Hardy'," he said, "but these guys are illiterate."

They all laughed. The easy banter was helping me relax. I looked ahead. Wendel was not wasting any time backtracking along the road. I could see dust in the headlights as he caught up to other trucks.

"Say, Wendel," the first Hardy called to the front, "did you wet yourself again? It's kind of smelly back here."

I answered him. "It's me," I said loud enough so all could hear. "I forgot to wiz in my hurry to depart so I tried squirting into the thermos in flight, but I think I got more on me."

There was a pause as they looked at each other, then they all burst out laughing.

"Well it's not easy," I continued in a mock seriousness. "You try holding a thermos, peeing and flying at the same time."

They laughed louder. Then I described what I did when the thermos was getting full and how I tried to empty the cup out the window.

"So what's the inside of the airplane smell like?" Twin number two asked between laughs.

"You can find out from Rocky in the morning," I replied. "He wants to fly over the job before I head home."

"He won't mind," Wendel offered. "He's got seven kids at home and I think most of them are still in diapers."

"Ya," twin one said, "he says that diapers are cheaper than real clothes."

They laughed again.

"If you don't have a thermos, how you supposed to pee in a plane?" someone asked.

"They got potties in them big planes," someone else replied, "but they're so tiny I had to stand in the aisle to have room."

"Sure, you wish but you lie," was one of the answers.

The dusty ride to the lodge lasted for half an hour. The laughter was continuous. We arrived at a big log building. I opened my door and popped out of the truck. I followed the men as they clomped up the wooden steps. The doors opened to a large room that served as a reception and dining area. It was filling with noisy construction workers.

"Hey everybody!" Wendel yelled. "Say 'Hi' to Stinky the pilot!"

Supper for the road crew that evening included mounds of beans and sprouts with stacks of thick steaks. Dessert was all-you-could-eat sugar pie. The banter died quickly as the workers tucked into their food. During coffee, my truck-riding buddies had me telling the story of peeing in the plane to the other workers. There must have been a shortage of new things to talk about in the bush camp. The laughter was loud and the comments kept it going.

"We could cut a hole in the floor of the plane fer your flight back," one of the men offered.

"Pierre says he just hangs it out the window and goes but nobody's seen him do it," another said.

"I don't have a choice," Pierre explained. "I could never fit mine in a thermos."

After more laughter and a few smokes, most of the workers headed to bed. They slept in tiny tourist cabins surrounding the lodge, four men in each. The lodge owner gave me an old mattress and a blanket. I carried them to the cabin with the Hardy Boys and their two buddies.

I was tired. It felt good to lie down but not for long. Between the lumpy mattress and eating too much, I could not get comfortable. Then the coffee and sugar pie started energizing my brain. I lay wide-awake. The other four were soon snoring loudly. A cool, damp breeze carried a symphony of snoring from the other cabins through the open windows. I

The breeze brought bad smells as the beans and sprouts did their work.

tossed and turned to keep warm and to redistribute the pain from the hard points of the mattress. Soon the breeze brought new noises and bad smells as the beans and sprouts did their work. Breathing through the musty blanket helped but I could not sleep.

Some time during the night, I heard Rocky return with the maintenance crew. It didn't seem long after when the cook banged the big metal triangle in front of the lodge. It was time to get up. The sky was still dark.

I washed as best I could but my teeth and clothes remained clammy. Breakfast was heart-stopping platters of eggs, ham, potatoes and pancakes. I ate less this time. The sky lightened on our way to the job site. Then the fog rolled in.

Rocky was already there. He had fuel in cans for me. "Good morning," he said cheerfully. "Did you get enough to eat? Did you sleep OK?" Before I could answer he continued. "This fog won't last. Check over your plane and gas it up so we can do a short flight as soon as it clears." He dropped the two cans and drove away in his truck.

The fog lifted soon after I had the airplane ready. The one trip over the job turned into three. I flew with the window open. No one complained about the smell in the back seat. Then I departed for home, stopping in Sudbury for more fuel. I cleaned up as best I could in the washroom at the Sudbury Airport. Then I took some wet paper towels out to the airplane and tried wiping up some of the residue on the inside. The moisture seemed to wake up the smell. I gave up and flew home with my side window open. It helped keep me awake.

Leanne was working behind the flight desk when I walked into The Flying Circus office.

"Welcome back, Charter Man," she said with a grin. Then she did a double take. "Wow! You look like you've been on an all-night bender."

"Thanks. It's nice to see you too."

She sniffed. "You don't smell very good."

"It's all part of the job," I replied. "I think teaching flying is easier than this charter stuff."

"I was picturing you relaxing and eating, all expenses paid, at a northern holiday resort. What happened?"

"Camp food and a hard mattress in a cold cabin in the bush with 20 windy construction workers are not my ideas of relaxing. The Petterson Construction people are nice but you can send Henry on their next flight north."

"Well, before you give up charter flying for good, we have a trip to Perth, near Ottawa." Without waiting for a reply, she added, "I thought you liked these flights so I already switched your students to Henry and Barry so you could take it."

I looked down at my soiled pants and then scratched my greasy hair. "Can I go home and shower first?"

"Yes," she laughed and sniffed. "A shower would be a good idea. Get some sleep too and maybe a change of clothes. The charter is for seven-thirty tomorrow morning."

"I'll have to clean the inside of the Citabria before I go," I said wearily.

"You're in luck. Charlie is here. He's cleaning a customer's airplane in the hangar. He'll do it for you."

"OK. Things are looking up."

Chainsaw Charlie was a 180-pound, muscular 14-year-old who washed and waxed airplanes for us after school and on Saturdays. He lived in the country on the other side of Circus with his mother and seven brothers and sisters. He loved to work and came to the airport whenever his mother wasn't using the family pickup truck.

Charlie's nickname was prompted by his backwoods talk and his lumberjack look. It stuck when he told us that he had built an airplane using scraps of plywood and an old chainsaw.

"She turned out heavier than Aunt May and a lot uglier," he grinned. "I tried to use 'er for a boat but she sank. Now she's the dock."

I walked out to the hangar and found Charlie working in the back.

"Hi there young fella," I said as I picked my way between the aircraft.

Charlie looked up, "Hi sir." He continued to scrub the customer's airplane.

"If you have time when you're finished here, Charlie, I have a big favour to ask."

The stocky kid straightened up as I approached. "I have some time," he replied. "What can I do for you?"

"I hate to ask but the inside of the Citabria needs cleaning."

"Someone lost their cookies again, did they?" he smiled knowingly.

"Not this time. It's worse."

He sniffed and frowned. "May I ask you a question, sir?"

"Sure, Charlie."

He stepped closer to me and spoke in a lowered voice. "Did you happen to wet yourself today, sir?"

"Actually, Charlie, no, I didn't."

"Oh," he said and hesitated, "if you don't mind me saying, sir, you smell like my little brothers when they're too many days between diaper changes."

"I don't mind you saying, Charlie. I didn't wet myself today, it was yesterday."

Chapter Seventeen

Elsemere 1; Government 0

L eanne had said that the morning charter was for two passengers in a
Cherokee. I was to fly them from Circus to the Smiths Falls Airport
for a meeting in nearby Perth, wait several hours and fly them back. It
seemed straightforward and held the promise of extra sleep while I was
waiting.

I drove home. My German Shepherd bounded up to the car when I
pulled into the driveway. I opened the driver's door. Her tail stopped wag-
ging. She sniffed my pants, sneezed and walked to the house. I let her in,
fed her and then sat on the couch for a minute.

Four hours later I was wakened by a cold dog nose nudging me. It was
dark and I was stiff. The dog wanted out. I got up, turned on some lights
and opened the door for her. I found something to eat, showered, watched
some television and went to bed.

I set my alarm for five-thirty. Sleep didn't come. I lay there checking
the clock frequently. The four-hour snooze had knocked my body clock
out of whack. I remembered looking at the time when it was three-thirty
and then the alarm went off.

I drove to work in the dark, made coffee and then checked over the
Cherokee at the front of the hangar. It was ready to go. I pulled it out and
started the engine. Everything worked.

My passengers arrived at sunrise, just before seven-thirty. The two
men were laughing at something as they climbed out of their car.

The driver was stocky, medium height and wide in the shoulders. He
looked like an ex-policeman whose physique was slipping from living the
good life. His sagging face held his mouth in a frown, which didn't dis-
appear when he laughed. He introduced himself as Randy Stewart.

"Mr. Stewart, pleased to meet you."

"Call me Randy," he said with a growl. "When I want you to call me

Mr. Stewart, I'll tell you." Then he laughed.

"Yes sir, Randy."

"And this is Dinty Elsemere," he said motioning toward the other man. "I call him Dingbat but then I pay him to take abuse."

Elsemere was taller, leaner and older than Stewart but his smile worked. I shook his hand.

"Pleased to meet you," I said.

"Likewise," Elsemere replied. "Call me Dinty or whatever you want."

Neither man was carrying a coat, luggage or a briefcase.

"I'm ready to go when you are, gentleman," I said, pointing to the open door of the Cherokee.

Randy rubbed his hands together as if to warm them and said, "Who's flying first?"

Elsemere laughed. They both looked at me.

"I'll take the first turn," I offered. I didn't know if they were joking or not. "If you don't mind?"

"Not at all," Randy replied. "Dinty, are you riding shotgun?"

"You go ahead," the older man said. "I'll sit in the back, further from the crash."

"Dint flew in the war," Randy explained. "He still thinks someone will be shooting at him when he gets in an airplane."

"Just don't let this madman fly and I'll be fine," Dinty replied.

We climbed in and took off. The weather was good. Cool, clear air made for a smooth ride. I followed the shoreline around the end of Lake Ontario on to Oshawa. From there I planned to follow the highways to Peterborough and then Smiths Falls.

Along the way I learned that both men liked to laugh. Randy enjoyed dropping into a gruff voice and saying off-the-wall things to catch people off guard.

He told me that he ran a toxic chemical clean-up company. "It's called 'Elsemere Environmental.' Dinty is my lawyer so I named the company after him," he declared with a laugh. "When my men make mistakes during a clean-up, the authorities demand to speak to Mr. Elsemere and end up talking to the company lawyer."

I laughed with him. Dinty smiled.

I offered them coffee from the thermos.

"Not for me," Dinty replied. "It goes right through me without stopping."

Randy produced a Mickey of scotch from his pocket. "I brought my own coffee," he declared. He took a swig from the bottle and then offered it to me.

"No thank you," I replied.

Randy explained that the purpose of their trip was to attend a demonstration of a chemical transfer process that his company had developed.

"We displace PCBs from electrical transformers with a non-toxic substitute without moving the unit. It's simpler, cheaper and safer. Some of those old transformers leak when you try to move them." Then he started to giggle and couldn't stop. It sounded funny coming from such a gruff-looking man.

Dinty leaned forward and continued the story. "Our men have set up a demonstration transfer inside the Perth Waterworks. The transformer stands between the two settling pools for the town's water supply."

Randy's giggle turned into guffaws. He tried to talk between outbursts. "The Environment... Minister requested... the demonstration... The numbskull has... no idea that it's..."

He was laughing too hard to finish the sentence. Dinty filled me in. "The Environment Minister is not happy that we developed a better transfer process than his own department. They have spent millions of dollars on removing transformers with men dressed like astronauts using special equipment and trucks." Randy laughed louder while nodding his head in agreement.

"They truck the units to a toxic waste site where they dump out the PCB but they never get it all. The residue mixes with the replacement liquid. When they have a spill during a removal, which is often, they call Randy's company to clean it up."

"Our process..." Randy squeaked as he laughed, "pumps new liquid in and pushes the PCB out..."

Dinty finished for him. "Randy's method saves time, money and spills but the government won't admit it's better than their big-dollar process."

Randy shook his head back and forth trying to catch his breath. "I get paid... either way... my transfer... or their spill."

"The minister granted us a one-time permit for this demonstration," Dinty explained. "He's stalling while his department figures out how it can discredit Randy's process."

"Why Perth?" I asked.

The question started Randy laughing again.

"Randy thinks the minister will have a fit," Dinty answered, "when he sees that the demonstration is set up beside the town water supply."

"So we're flying to Perth to see the reaction of the Minister of Environment?" I asked.

Randy laughed and nodded.

"We've also invited the national media," Dinty added, "and the minister doesn't know it. We want the public to see what we're doing before the government sweeps us under the carpet."

"OK, I think I get the picture," I smiled.

Randy continued to laugh.

I got busy talking on the radio along the Toronto shoreline. The air traffic controllers must have wondered about the giggling noise in my transmissions but they didn't ask. Randy eventually settled down. He and Dinty watched Toronto's downtown area slide by our left wing. Randy fell asleep after we had passed the built-up area.

"You're welcome to join us at the waterworks," Dinty offered.

"Thank you," I replied. "I'd like that. What are the chances of the media covering the demonstration?"

"Oh, they'll be there," Dinty declared. "The Ministry of Environment tried to discredit Randy's company before. He was accused of dumping PCBs in a public garbage site. Randy told them that he had disposed of the rusted tanks off two sewage-pumping trucks at that site. They didn't believe him so they paid to have the dump excavated. While the digging was going on, Randy was interviewed on national TV news. The interviewer said, 'Tell me Mr. Stewart, what will they find in those tanks when they get to the bottom?'

"Randy gave a one-word answer. He said, 'Pooh.'

"The interviewer replied, 'Pardon me?'

"Randy said, 'They'll find rusted septic tanks crusted with poop!'

"After all the expense, that's exactly what they found. Since then, the media show up whenever he calls."

"I'm sorry I missed that one."

I asked Dinty if they were being met at the airport.

"No, we'll need a taxi," he replied.

There was no control tower at Smiths Falls so I called on the unicom advisory frequency. An older man's voice responded and acknowledged my request for a cab. It made me feel like an efficient charter pilot to be thinking ahead for my passengers.

Our flightpath along Highway 7 took us over Perth, so I throttled back and descended early. The drop in engine noise woke up Randy. I pointed to the city over the Cherokee's nose.

"Perth," I declared. Randy nodded his understanding. He rubbed the sleep from his face and then drew a circle in the air with his finger. "Can we fly around the city?"

I turned right until Randy found the waterworks building with his pump truck parked outside. "It looks like they're set up," he announced.

I turned toward the Smiths Falls Airport and flew overhead the single paved strip before joining a left downwind for Runway 24. I made blind position reports on the unicom frequency. There were no replies.

As we were taxiing in, a black limousine pulled into the parking lot.

"Nice cab," Dinty said.

"That'll be for the minister and his group," Randy replied, looking at his watch. "They'll be landing soon."

I pulled over to the edge of the empty ramp and shut down the engine. We climbed out.

"My legs may never recover," Dinty said, unbending himself slowly.

"We can put Randy in the back for the return flight," I suggested.

"I'll live," Dinty replied.

"Yeah but he'll complain," Randy said with a chuckle.

As I was locking the door on the Cherokee, a thin, older man dressed in worn work clothes walked out of a clubhouse and headed our way. He was so bowlegged that he looked like a cartoon cowboy. He raised his hand and opened his mouth as if to call to us but the sound did not make it across the ramp. When he was closer, I realized that he was shouting quietly as if his old throat was parched.

"You can't park there," he rasped.

Now he tells me, I thought. He could have said something on the radio about parking or he could have directed us when we taxied in. I looked around at the empty ramp. "Why not?" I asked semi-politely.

He swallowed hard, but it didn't help his sandpaper voice. "A government plane is coming," he wheezed. "It'll be parking there."

Before I could reply, Randy spoke for me. "Where would you like us to park?" he asked in a friendly tone.

"Over there," the old-timer grumbled. He pointed to a grass area on the other side of the ramp.

"Then tell the government pilot to park over there and we'll stay put," Randy replied. He tried to smile but it just distorted his down-turned face. "We're taxpayers."

The airport geezer looked him over and then said gruffly, "Next you'll want a washroom and then a ride into town."

"I thought you were calling a cab?" Randy countered.

The older man stuck his chin out defiantly. "I was gonna give you a lift myself but now you can walk and I hope you wet your pants."

Randy didn't miss a beat. This man was talking his language. "I'd be happy to piss on the grass where the government is going to park," he replied. As he spoke, he dug out a roll of bills from a pocket. "But I still need to get to Perth. Is fifty bucks enough apology for being so rude to a man who was going to be a friend?"

"Fifty will help," the cowboy replied hoarsely. "It might buy you a ride; one way."

Randy chuckled. "I like your style, old man," He peeled off several large bills.

The cowboy took the money and counted it. "My pleasure city boy. Now let's go. I wanna be back for the next plane."

"As soon as I relieve myself," Randy replied.

He walked across the ramp to the open area of grass and watered it.

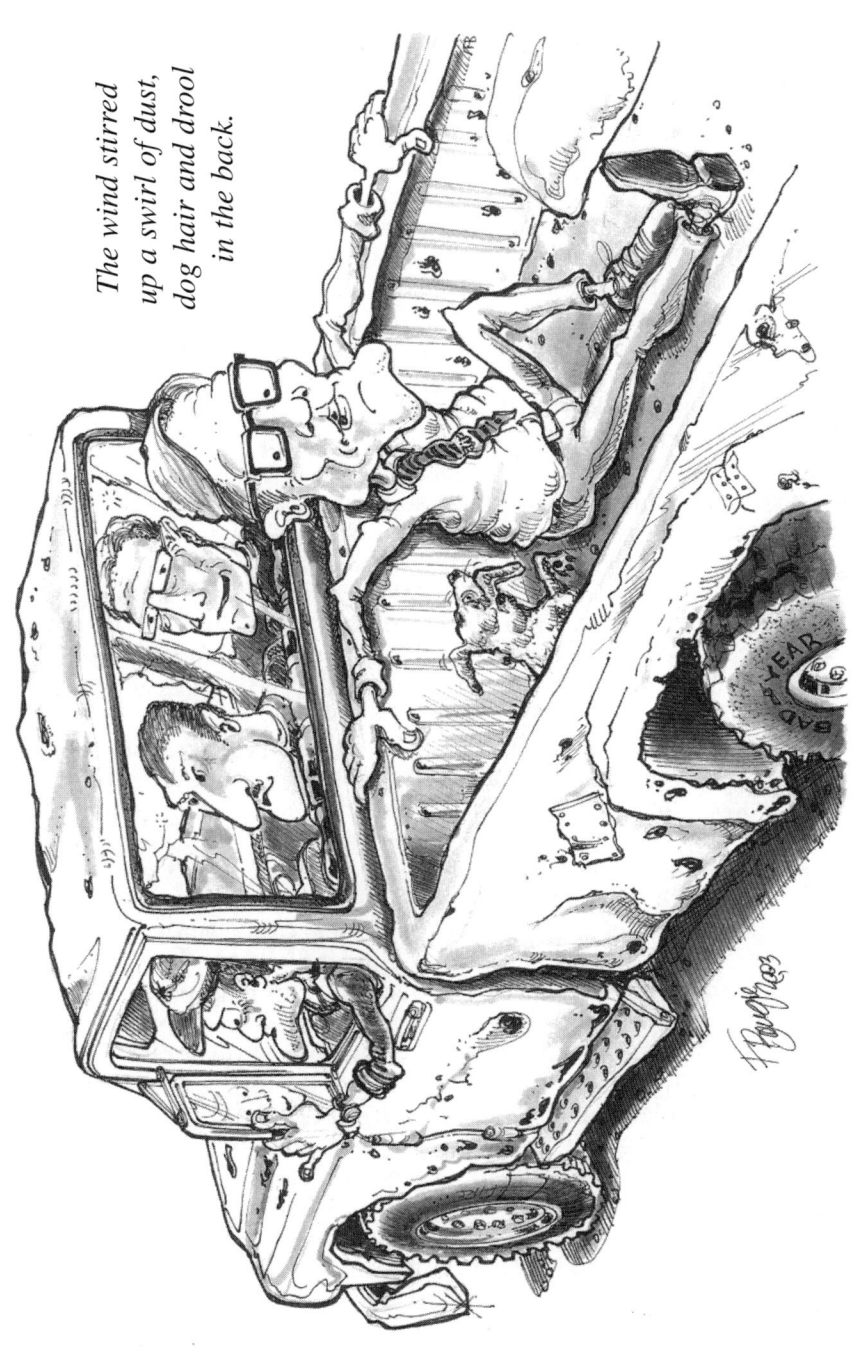

*The wind stirred
up a swirl of dust,
dog hair and drool
in the back.*

"Youse two can use the washroom inside if you like," the older man said motioning toward the clubhouse, "while we're waiting for your friend to hose his shoes."

"Don't mind if I do," Dinty smiled.

The only other vehicle around was a dilapidated pickup truck. "Is this our ride?" I asked, pointing to the truck.

Our reluctant host stopped and turned. "What of it?"

"Nothing, I love trucks," I said quickly.

I volunteered to ride in the back so Randy and Dinty could sit up front with our chauffeur. I knew it would be cool but the worst part was the dog. I saw an old black and grey mutt sleeping in the truck bed when I started to climb in.

"Pay no mind to Hash," the cowboy said.

I tiptoed around the beast and sat with my back to the cab. The mutt stared at me and drooled as if I was in his space. I wondered if he was one of those dogs trained to let strangers in but not out. The truck roared off. The wind stirred up a swirl of dust, dog hair and drool in the back.

I was well blown and gritty when the squeal of brakes on the old pick-up announced our arrival at the Perth Waterworks. I hopped over the side opposite the dog and slapped a cloud of dust off my clothes. Once more, I thought to myself, I'd be returning from a charter trip dirty and smelly.

Randy, Dinty and the driver climbed out of the front seat smiling and laughing like they were old friends.

A larger, flatbed truck with an arrangement of tanks, pumps, panels and hoses was parked near a door on the side of the old brick building. The truck was painted all white except the green lettering on the driver's door, "Elsemere Environmental."

Randy waved to our chauffeur as he roared off. "Let's go in the front and see if everything's ready."

I followed as the two men walked through the waterworks entrance. Inside was a small, unoccupied office. Beyond, another door opened into a large room dominated by two mid-sized swimming pools mounted in the floor. A two-metre wide tiled space ran between them with a raised wooden platform at the far end. A dark green electrical transformer, like the ones on hydro poles, sat on the platform. It was a serious looking unit with heavy insulators and cables sticking out of the top. There were two hoses running from it, across the nearest pool and out the side door. The room echoed with the steady hum of electric pumps.

Five men dressed in work clothes were standing and talking near the hoses. We walked the length of the pool to greet them. Two were Randy's men, two were from the waterworks and the last was introduced as a local hydro inspector.

Five or six newspaper reporters and a television crew were the next to arrive via the front entrance. Dinty and I stood back while they looked at the setup and talked to Randy.

At ten minutes to 11:00, Randy nodded to his men to get ready. They both went outside. One returned trailing an electric cable wired to a switch box. He spoke to the hydro guy who walked over to a panel and killed the power. The hum of pumps in the building slowed to a stop. It was replaced by the noise of the generator idling outside on the truck.

At five minutes to 11:00, four men in dark suits walked in. They took quick strides to our end of the room. Randy shook hands with the leader who must have been the Environment Minister. He was the heaviest and best dressed. None of them looked like they had ridden in the back of a farm truck to get there. Randy pointed out the transformer for them and signaled his worker.

The Elsemere man pushed a button on his handheld control box. The noise of a pump starting came from the truck followed by the sound of the generator revving up. The first three metres of hose running in and out of the transformer were clear plastic. The worker opened a valve where the top hose connected to the transformer. Green liquid started to flow toward the transformer. He opened a valve on the bottom hose. A darker liquid from the transformer appeared in it.

One of the government people leaned close to the minister and spoke into his ear. The minister's face reddened. He hailed Randy who was not far away. He had to shout but he was trying to yell quietly so that Randy was the only one to hear him. Randy listened and nodded while the minister ranted and waved at the pools, hoses and transformer. The TV cameraman was filming them. I caught parts of the conversation. He told Randy that the setup was too dangerous and should be shut down.

Randy replied in agreement. "That's why this is the best way for the transfer." His voice boomed loud and clear for everyone. "To move that unit for an off-site transfer would require draining the pools and closing this place for a week and that's only if there was no spill."

The minister pointed to the water and started to reply. At the same time, Randy's worker shut off the valves and killed the pump. The transfer was finished. The noise level dropped in time for us to hear the minister say, "...is the only operation that should be used in this situation!"

I think he was referring to the government removal method but we didn't hear that part. Before the minister could say more, the TV newsman stepped forward holding a microphone.

"Tell us sir, what does the government think of this method of PCB removal from transformers?"

The minister sputtered a little and then said, "Well it certainly warrants further study. We will be looking into it." He turned and walked out. His men followed.

Randy stepped in front of the camera and expounded on the virtues of his transfer method. The newspaper reporters stood behind the camera and took notes. When the TV crew said they had enough coverage, the media packed up and left.

Randy was excited. He considered this a victory for his company. "The least they'll do is schedule more demonstrations on temporary permits," he said to Dinty and me. "We'll keep the pressure on by asking why the government is delaying full authority for us to rid the province of PCBs."

He walked over and thanked the waterworks and hydro guys for their help. His men were disconnecting the hoses from the transformer.

"Once you're done here," he declared, "I'm buying lunch for everyone, that is, if you name the place and give us a ride."

It sounded good to me. Hunger combined with my lack of sleep was making me light-headed.

Lunch was at a tavern in town. I rode in the back of a public works pickup truck but it wasn't for long and there was no drooling dog.

A poster beside the entrance to the bar declared that this was "Busty Bell Week." The advertisement declared that Busty sported measurements of 80-28-34.

"Maybe they're just two forties," Randy said with a laugh.

"No, they're not," one of the waterworks guys replied.

He was right. When my eyes had adjusted to the smoky darkness, I could see a bikini-clad dancer on a small stage that jutted into the room. The music was rocking and the large babe had a pair of big boobs rolling. The bikini was straining.

The place was busy but not packed. Randy led us to a table near the stage. I sat as far away from the action as I could. A waitress came right over. I ordered a cola.

Randy caught Busty's eye. The dancer gyrated and watched while he pulled out a twenty-dollar bill from his pocket. Before I realized what he was doing, he reached over and stuffed it in the neck of my shirt. The big woman continued to dance. Another $20 came out. This one he stuffed into my shirt pocket. That made Busty smile. I didn't protest since the guys at our table and most of the people in the room were now watching Busty and me.

Randy pulled out another $20 but held on to it. Busty slinked off the stage and danced toward our table. She rubbed against each man that she passed but she kept her eyes on Randy while heading toward me. Randy reached over and stuffed the bill into the front of my pants.

Busty looked bigger and older up close. She wrapped herself around me and pulled my face into her chest. My nose filled with the smell of sweat mixed with cheap perfume. She held on to me while walking her

Busty looked bigger up close.

lips down the side of my head. I held my breath. The crowd whistled and cheered as she plucked the first bill from my neck with her teeth. She pulled back, grabbed the money from her mouth and stuck it inside her panties. The crowd began a rhythmic clapping. Busty continued by bending over and wiggling her lips down my shirt, pulling out the next bill with her lips. The clapping speeded up. I could feel my face burning.

For the last one, she kneeled beside me and buried her face in the top of my pants. The crowd roared. I looked at Randy. He was leaning back in his chair clapping and laughing. Busty popped up with the final twenty in her mouth. She tucked it away and then turned to Randy. She grabbed him to her chest, squeezed and released him before planting a big kiss on his cheek. She danced toward the back wall, waved to the crowd and disappeared through a door beside the stage.

Randy was laughing so hard he couldn't talk. I sat there willing the crowd to ignore us. The waitress arrived with our drinks. She handed them around the table and then asked for our food order. When it was my turn, Randy took a deep breath and stopped laughing for a moment. "He'll have watermelon; two of them." He roared with laughter again.

The waitress smiled. "We don't have watermelon. What can I get for you?"

I gave her my order. Randy was still laughing.

"He'll have the same," I said.

I sipped my cola until Randy started to settle down. "I thought you were going to die in there," he laughed. "I think she pulled you out just in time. The look on your red face was better than the minister's at the waterworks. It was worth the sixty bucks!"

Our meals came. I had ordered the sausage special.

Randy looked at his and said, "What's this?"

"Bangers and mash," Dinty replied before I could say anything.

The name started Randy laughing all over again.

The food helped me stay awake but by the time we were riding a taxi back to the airport, my lack of sleep was catching up to me. I nodded off a couple of times.

Our cowboy friend came out of the clubhouse when the cab pulled up beside the Cherokee. "May we buy some fuel?" I asked.

"Got money?" he replied.

I produced a credit card.

"Nope, that's plastic; money is paper with numbers on it. The bigger the numbers, the better."

Randy pulled out his roll of cash.

"Yeah, like that stuff," the ramp man said. "Pull your plane over and we'll fill 'er up."

"Thanks, Randy," I said. "I'll knock the cost off your charter bill."

"It beats walking," he laughed.

We were ready to go. Randy climbed into the back seat, curled up and went right to sleep. Dinty sat up front with me. Once we had taken off and reached cruising altitude, I asked the older man if he wanted to fly.

"Don't mind if I do," he replied.

The air was mostly smooth. It was obvious that Dinty had flown before. He held the controls lightly and didn't overcorrect for the little turbulence there was.

"Just follow that highway," I said, pointing to the road snaking through the bush below. Then I leaned my head against my side window. The vibration in the Plexiglas massaged my temple. I was asleep in a minute.

I woke up with a start. The engine noise was changing. I looked around wildly trying to figure out where I was. My heart skipped a few beats and then began pounding. I focused on the strange man beside me.

"I need to use the facilities," Dinty explained calmly as he reduced the power and set up a descent.

I looked forward. The Peterborough Airport was ahead and below.

"Is there someone we should be calling on the RT?" Dinty asked.

"Yes," I replied. There was no control tower at Peterborough but I looked up the traffic advisory frequency, switched the radio and called in a position report. Someone on the ground responded giving us Runway 27 as the active.

Dinty seemed to know what to do. He set the airplane up for an overhead arrival to a downwind leg for the runway. I let him continue flying.

"What is the pattern height," he asked.

"Sixteen hundred feet," I replied.

I radioed from overhead the airport while Dinty leveled off at the right altitude and looked around for traffic. The man must have watched and memorized what I had done on the way to Smiths Falls. He turned onto the downwind leg and went through a pre-landing check.

"Did I miss anything?" he asked.

"No."

The older man continued the approach, setting up the proper speed and flaps for a landing. He looked at me expectantly.

"You're doing fine," I said. "Keep going."

The former wartime pilot didn't need any more prompting. He flew the Cherokee to a perfect landing. It was so smooth that Randy did not wake up. Dinty parked in front of the small terminal building and shut down the engine.

"I enjoyed that," Dinty said to me. "Thank you very much."

"You're welcome. I'm embarrassed that I fell asleep."

"I'm glad you did," Dinty replied. "It was a wonderful opportunity to fly again."

"How long has it been since your last time?"

He smiled, "Nineteen forty-six."

We woke Randy and the three of us went to the washroom in the terminal building. Randy bought a round of sodas from a machine and we walked back to the airplane. Randy opted for the back seat again. I offered Dinty the pilot seat on the left side. "Most of my flying is instructing from the right side," I explained.

"All right, thank you."

He started the Cherokee's engine and taxied out. He completed the cockpit checks without missing a thing. I worked the communication radio. Randy fell asleep. We took off and headed for Oshawa and then followed the north shore of Lake Ontario along Toronto's waterfront.

When we were clear of the high traffic area, I asked Dinty what types of aircraft he had flown in the war.

"I finished my last tour flying photo recon on Mosquitos. It was a good airplane. It could fly higher and faster than the fighter aircraft of the day but it was a handful. Loaded, its stall speed was higher than our cruise speed now."

"Have you ever considered getting back into flying?"

"Not for long. I enjoyed flying but war is hell. I lost a lot of friends in aircraft. I was glad when it ended and we could all be civilized again."

"You fly very well."

"Thank you. I wouldn't mind doing this again but that's as far as I would go."

It was five o'clock when we landed at Circus. Dinty and Randy went into the office with me. Dinty went to the washroom. Summer McDay was working behind the desk.

"Good afternoon gentlemen," Summer said cheerfully, "did you have a good flight?"

"It was great," Randy replied giving the young college student a thorough inspection, "but my partner did most of the flying. Do I get a discount for that?"

"Sounds like a lesson," Summer replied with a grin. "I'll have to charge extra."

Randy looked to me for a response. It was the first time I had seen him lost for words.

"He gets a discount, but it's for the fuel he purchased for us. I'll finish the charter sheet and then you can make out Mr. Stewart's bill."

"Fine," Summer replied holding her big smile.

Randy leaned on the counter to be closer to her. "What's a nice little girl like you doing in a place like this?" he leered while showing his best, crooked grin.

"Well sir, I'm not little and as far as you know, I may not be a girl."

Randy roared with laughter. "I'm game... any time you want... to show me," he said between laughs.

"I think you're old enough to be my father," she replied.

"Could be," Randy said with another laugh. "What was your mother's maiden name?"

I interrupted them before Summer had a chance to out-duel our customer. "Here are the numbers for the charter," I said.

Randy pulled out his money roll and paid cash. He offered me his hearty handshake. "That was a great trip," he declared.

"I'm glad it worked well for you," I replied.

I was tired and thinking it would be good to get back to the routine of instructing.

"We'll do it again soon," he said to me and then turned toward Summer. "When I call for the next charter, make sure I get this guy for my pilot."

"OK dad!"

Chapter Eighteen

The Blue Goose

Henry flew Olaf Petterson to an equipment auction in Sudbury. It was evening before he returned. I had spent a busy day teaching my students and his. I had forgotten how much energy it took to fly with pilots who didn't know what they were doing.

I had just finished fueling, cleaning and pushing the other airplanes into the hangar when Henry taxied onto The Flying Circus ramp.

"Good timing, partner," I said when he shut down the engine and opened the door on the Cherokee. "Did you have a good trip?"

He gave me the normal Henry response. "Yes," he replied but he was grinning more than usual.

"What happened?"

"Petterson bought an airplane," he answered calmly.

"What? Where? What airplane?"

"He bought an Aero Commander at the equipment auction."

"You're kidding!" This was sounding exciting. I knew that Aero Commander had manufactured everything from single-engine airplanes to business jets. "What kind of Aero Commander?"

"An AC-560," Henry replied.

The 500 series of Commanders were piston-powered, twin-engine aircraft but I had never heard of a 560.

"So tell me more. What does it look like? Where is it? Are we going to fly it?"

"Well, if you help me gas this thing and put it away, I'll tell you what I know."

Henry pumped fuel while I cleaned the Cherokee's windshield and wing leading edges. He said that the Commander was an early version of the twin-engine 500 series. "This one was built in 1956," he said. "You enter the cabin through a side door behind the left wing. There is a bench seat at the back for three passengers, or two construction workers, and two seats against a cockpit partition facing rearward. You walk between them to access two seats in the cockpit."

Henry said the airplane looked rough. "It fit in well with the used construction equipment."

"What possessed Petterson to buy it?"

"I'm not sure. He was there to purchase road-building equipment, which he did. When the bidding got to the airplane, he asked me if it might be something he could use. I said, 'Maybe.'

"The auctioneer tried to start at fifty thousand dollars but there were no takers. Petterson bid five thousand. One other guy ran him up to eight and it was his."

"Wow! This is our entry to big-time flying," I declared.

"We'll see. It might need more repairs than it's worth," Henry cautioned, "but it has a current Certificate of Airworthiness and was flown in for the auction."

"Is Petterson already committed to the sale?"

"Oh yes, the airplane is his. Now we see if it's really flyable or if it goes for scrap. I'll call Darcy in the morning and see when he can check it over."

Three days later, Henry flew to Derry, picked up Darcy Phillips and continued north to inspect Petterson's impromptu purchase. Darcy was the chief of maintenance at Derry Air, an air service not far from Circus. His shop maintained our aircraft on a contract.

I flew with students all that day. They careened through the sky; I daydreamed. My mind wasn't really in a Cherokee. It was piloting a cabin-class business aircraft.

I was debriefing the last student when a heavy rumble of engines interrupted us. It sounded as if several large aircraft were taxiing toward The Flying Circus office. The throaty noise grew louder and was joined by the heavy squeal of brakes as the aircraft turned onto our ramp. I stood up and looked out the window expecting to see a World War II bomber.

It was an Aero Commander. Two large engines and the fuselage were mounted under a high wing that stretched to both sides of the ramp. The bottom of the fuselage sat low to the ground. The main landing gear hung below the engines. The whole airplane was painted in a faded medium blue colour broken by white stripes running horizontally along the fuselage.

The airplane parked in front of our hangar. The throbbing exhaust noise was replaced by a metallic clatter as the propellers wound down and stopped turning. I recognized the face peering over the top of the instrument panel from the pilot's seat. It was Darcy.

I invited my student to come out with me and see the airplane. As we approached, the left side door opened and the wiry little mechanic hopped onto the tarmac. He opened an access panel behind the door and pulled out two undercarriage pins attached to red streamers.

"Hi Darcy, so this is it?"

He closed the hatch and turned our way. "Hey, it's The Flying Circus clown," he said with a grin. "How're tricks today?" He ducked his head under the left engine nacelle to insert one of the pins.

"Where's Henry?" I asked.

His answer echoed from inside the wheelwell. "He's behind me in the Cherokee." He popped his head out and walked around the nose toward the landing gear on the other side.

"You flew this by yourself?"

He answered in a singsong sarcastic voice. "Did you think that aircraft mechanics can't fly?"

"No."

"Good," he barked while inserting the other pin.

"I didn't know you had a multi-engine aircraft endorsement."

"Who said I did?" he replied. He approached my student. "Hi, I'm Darcy Phillips."

I introduced them.

"Pleased to meet you," Darcy said. "Before this guy tells fairy tales about aircraft mechanics, you should know that the most dangerous thing in aviation is a flying instructor with a screwdriver."

"Now tell him how you fly a twin-engine aircraft on a single-engine pilot licence," I suggested. For once I was hoping to get the better of the jokester mechanic.

"One engine at a time," Darcy grinned in reply. "I alternated left and right engines all the way here so one leg wouldn't get tired holding the course straight with rudder."

"Then why were both engines running when you arrived?" I asked.

"A Commander's nosewheel steering is dampened with hydraulics, smart guy. It won't taxi straight on one engine. Besides, taxiing isn't flying."

I let it drop before Darcy could fill my student with more bad ideas.

"May we look inside?" my student asked.

"Help yourself." Darcy waved us toward the open door. "Just don't let this clown show you how the landing gear retracts."

We walked around the left engine and ducked under the outboard wing.

"He doesn't seem to like you much," my student said in a low voice.

"Oh we get along fine," I replied. "Darcy spears everyone he likes."

"Then I don't want to hear what he says to people he hates."

"Me either."

We stepped inside and sat on the rear bench seat. The cabin looked like a museum for furnishings from the early 1950s. Two-tone, pleated blue fabric covered the round bulky seats. Heavy chrome ashtrays swiveled down from the cabin sidewalls. Everything was a little dirty, but not torn or shabby.

I led the way forward walking in a squat. I tried different contortions before I found the combination that got me over the centre console and into the pilot's seat. I invited my student to sit on the right side.

The seats were big and comfortable once you got into them. The cockpit smelled like I imagined a big old airplane should: a mixture of avgas, grease, oil, mold, dust and maybe a little sweat. The control wheels on each side were attached to heavy metal columns that arched over to the sidewalls and disappeared into a slot in the floor. Everything on the instrument panel had a heavy, military look. Each instrument was hooded with eyebrow lighting. The knobs and switches protruded from the panel. The radios were awkwardly positioned low on each side behind the control wheels.

Looking outside through the windshields, the visibility was excellent. The pilots sat close to the nose which dropped away sharply.

Darcy walked up to the front wheel carrying the tow bar from our hangar. We climbed out while he clamped it on.

"Help me turn this thing around," he said. "We can park it right here facing out."

"How about in the hangar?" I suggested. "We can charge more rent if we store it there."

"How wide is your opening?"

I thought for a moment. "Forty-five feet," I replied.

"The Commander's wing span is forty-four feet plus the nav lights," Darcy said as he walked to the front of the tow bar. "Are you feeling lucky today?"

"No."

"Then both of you push on the base of a prop blade on my right side."

I caught sight of the registration on the Commander for the first time. "Golf Oscar Oscar Sierra," I said out loud. "The goose, the Blue Goose."

The three of us moved the big airplane, but just barely.

"Darcy," I said between grunts, "is this thing airworthy?"

"I flew it here, didn't I?" he replied as we backed the Commander around.

"So when do we start flying it?"

"Not today. Now pull on the other side," he directed. "I know a guy who can check you out. I'll call him when I get home."

"Wait a minute," I replied. "Who checked you out on the Aero Com-

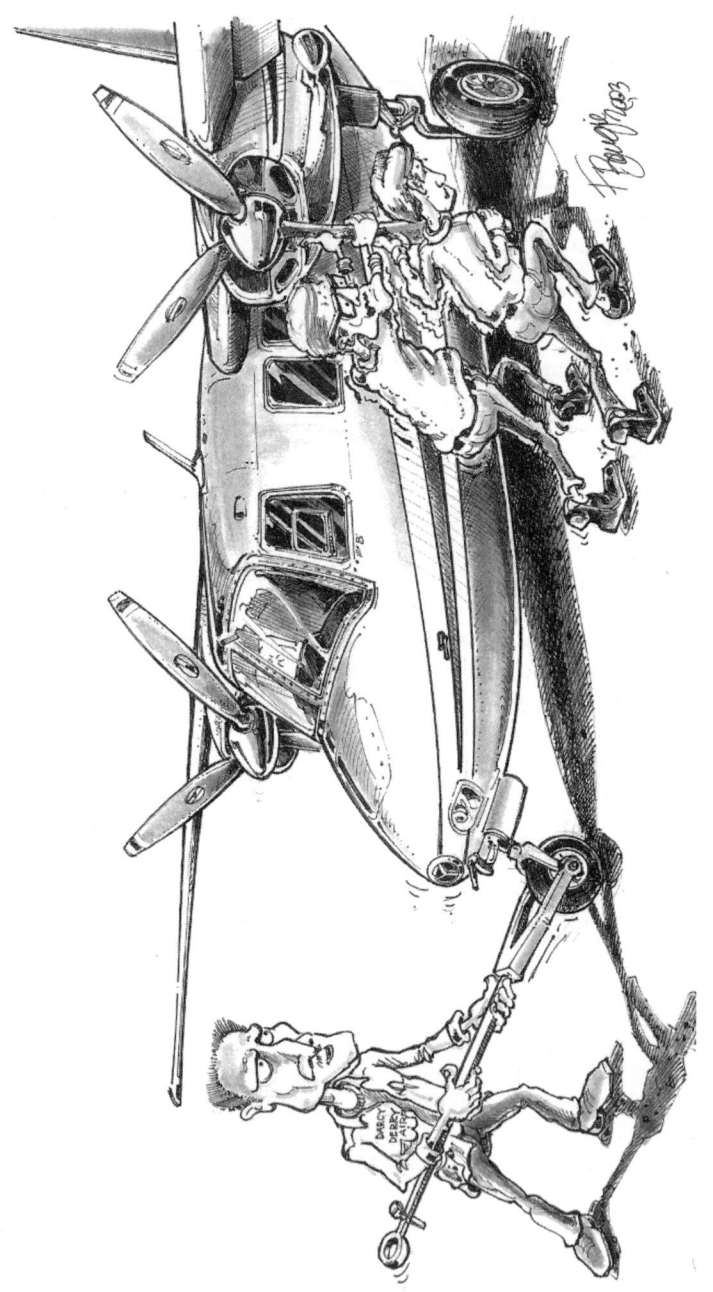

Darcy walked to the front of the tow bar. "Are you feeling lucky today?"

mander?"

"Same guy."

"Where does he live?"

"Near Derry," the mechanic said with a sly grin. "Now let's have one of you pushing on each side." Then he added, "He checked me out on the telephone."

"If it's that easy, we can fly this to Derry and you can check me on the way. I'll drop you off and fly back."

"No thanks," he replied. "I'm a mechanic, not a magician."

Chapter Nineteen

Ziggy Burns

Darcy returned to Derry in a Cherokee that was coming up for an inspection. The forecast for the next day was a preview of winter's upcoming season. Low cloud, rain and freezing rain were to sweep through the area.

It was Henry and Leanne's turn to take a bad-weather day off. I drove through the wet weather to the office. I called customers, cancelled their lessons and arranged future bookings. Then I put my feet up, watched the rain change to freezing rain and opened the pilot manual for the Blue Goose.

"Congratulations on your purchase of the 1956 Aero Commander 560 A-HC," the first page trumpeted. Underneath was a black and white photo of the airplane with five people dressed in 1950's business attire walking away from the open cabin door.

The handbook described an airplane that delivered easy loading, cabin-class comfort and low noise. It claimed that the complexities found in other twin-engine aircraft had been simplified. Some of the features listed were: single-point refueling, single-point fuel selection, automatic mixture control, the latest Century autopilot, hydraulics run directly from a hydraulic pump, and electrics run by a generator.

I finished reading the manual and was starting to daydream about being an executive pilot when the telephone rang.

"Is this the Sliding Circus?" It was Darcy.

"More like the Silent Circus today. There's not much going on."

"Well, your inspection is done. We'll arrange delivery or pickup when the weather clears."

"Thank you. I'm glad someone is making money today."

"I thought flying school owners arrange for weather like this so they can count the dollars that pile up."

"We don't keep it long enough to count it, smart guy."

"I spoke to Ziggy Burns about checking you and Henry out on the Blue Goose. He's available tomorrow. Can you guys swing that?"

"We could but only because everything is coated with ice. It isn't safe to walk out there let alone fly."

"I'll give you his number. He's home now but he won't call you. He doesn't like spending money phoning. Actually, he doesn't like spending money on anything. You guys should get along fine."

I wrote down the name and phone number. "Thanks, Darcy."

"Any time. I aim to keep you guys flying so I'll be in business forever."

I punched in Ziggy Burns' number and was greeted abruptly on the first ring.

"Burns."

"Ziggy Burns?"

"Yes," the voice answered curtly.

"I'm calling from The Flying Circus, Darcy Phi..."

"I can be there tomorrow, nine o'clock."

"Well, we may not be able to fly because of the ice."

"No problem, I'll see you tomorrow."

"Click." He had hung up.

I called Henry at home and told him we were on with a Commander check-pilot named Ziggy Burns the next day for at least a ground briefing. Then I did some paperwork, ate my lunch and flipped through the Commander's handbook again.

The telephone rang a couple of times. One call was from the Circus Airport Manager, Barney Swallow.

"The airport's closed," he wheezed.

"Thanks for letting me know, Barney. I guess it's slippery out there. How does it look for tomorrow?"

"Ask me tomorrow."

"OK. Take care going home."

"I am home. Only a fool would be out there today."

"Whatever you say, Barney."

Only fools and flying school owners, I thought to myself.

I left the office early but arrived home late after crawling along with the traffic in freezing rain.

The next day dawned clear and cold. The hardest part of getting to work was sliding to my car and beating the ice off it with my fist so I could get to the scraper inside. The streets had been salted into useable tracks. Even the airport entrance road had been sanded and salted lightly, something that skinflint Barney loathed doing. "It rusts the truck and kills the grass," Barney would grumble, "and we have to sweep it up in the spring."

Henry had arrived at The Flying Circus ahead of me and had sprinkled some ice-melter on the walk. I looked at the ramp and taxiway as I shuffled toward the office. In the foreground, the Commander sat like a large, glazed, blueberry-coloured birthday cake. Icicles hung from the edges of the wings and tail. The asphalt was a skating rink.

"Good morning," I said to Henry as I opened the office door.

"Hi there. Thanks for covering for us yesterday," he replied.

"You're welcome. The weather looks good but the airport doesn't."

"Barney has issued a Notice to Airmen closing everything."

"I'll talk to him. The Commander looks like a no-go but the airplanes in the hangar are flyable."

"You'll be wasting your time. I already cancelled our first student."

"It's worth a try."

I called the airport office. Barney answered. "Airport."

"Good morning Barney. Thanks for salting the entrance road."

"It's bad for the environment."

"Yes, but so are wrecked cars in the ditch."

"What can I do for you?" he grumbled.

"Can we get some sand on the runway so we can fly?"

"Hot sand costs too much."

"The airport's closed," he replied.

"Well, it wouldn't have to be if the runways and taxiways were sand-ed."

"The sand will just blow off with that wind."

"Didn't you say the county has heated sand for windy days?"

"It costs too much."

"Come on, Barney, that's what your budget is for; spend money to cre-ate activity."

"You give me $1,200 and I'll spread hot sand on the main runway. Until then the airport is closed."

"Are you waiting for spring?"

"The sun is out. The ice will melt."

"It's ten degrees below freezing. It won't melt," I argued.

"Then we'll wait until it sublimates."

Henry had been right, I was wasting my time. It was Barney's way or the highway.

I hung up the phone and looked outside in time to see an old Volk-swagen Rabbit dogtrack into our parking lot. It looked like a wounded airplane landing in a crosswind. The car leaned right, pointed left and went straight. It was trailing black smoke.

"Do you suppose this is Darcy's man?" I asked Henry.

My partner stood up from behind the desk.

A short, skinny guy dressed like a scarecrow stepped out of the car.

"Oh, it could be, knowing Darcy."

The visitor limped briskly toward the office. He walked as if one leg was shorter than the other and it was trying to catch up. An old school binder stuffed fat with loose paper was tucked under one arm. Mr. Scare-crow was dressed in a moth-eaten grey cardigan with patches of faded plaid shirt showing through the holes. A bony left knee poked through a thin spot in his blue jeans. Below the pants, sockless feet shuffled inside a pair of over-sized penny loafers. It made me cold to look at him.

I opened the office door as he came up the walk. Up close it was impossible to tell the man's age.

"Good morning," I said cheerfully.

He looked up at the sky and then back to me. "I guess it is now," he answered with a little smile.

I stuck out my hand and introduced myself.

"Ziggy Burns," he replied, accepting the handshake.

"This is my partner, Henry Rains," I said as Henry came around the desk.

"Welcome to The Flying Circus," Henry said warmly. They shook hands.

"Darcy speaks highly of you," I offered.

The smile on the lean pilot's face spread into a crooked grin. "I won't say what he told me about you."

"I can imagine," I replied.

"Would you like some coffee?" Henry asked, pointing toward the pot on the burner.

"Is it free?" the little man asked.

"On the house," Henry replied, "but I'll warn you that my partner made it."

"Help yourself," I added. "Do we call you Ziggy or Captain Burns."

"Call me anything you like," he said making his way to the coffeemaker. "'Ziggy' is good. It works better during a cockpit fire than calling me 'Burns'." He grinned at his own joke.

"Is it true that you checked Darcy out over the phone?" I asked.

Ziggy by-passed the Styrofoam cups and reached down for a staff mug. He poured some coffee into it and then added two heaping spoons of sugar and a steady stream of creamer.

Henry and I poured our own coffees and invited this strange pilot to sit at a briefing table.

"How do we start?" Henry asked.

"I teach by the day for cash," he answered. "The lesson starts now and ends when I leave with my money."

"Understood," Henry replied. "We're ready when you are."

"Good." He sipped some coffee and then carefully opened his tattered binder.

I was thinking we didn't need to pay for a whole day if we couldn't fly. "Is it true that you checked Darcy on this Commander over the telephone?" I asked.

Burns gave me a hard look for a moment. His left leg began jiggling up and down. He pushed on the knee with his left hand but the leg continued to bounce, making his head rock slightly.

"Darcy is the smartest aircraft mechanic in the world," he said calmly but firmly, "but he is impossible to teach. He has to learn everything for himself. I suggested a few things to him over the phone and he figured out the rest, at least I assume he did. It looks like the airplane is here."

"It is," I answered.

"Is that the kind of checkout you're looking for?" our instructor asked.

"No," Henry said quickly.

His jumpy leg settled down. "So we'll start with a ground briefing," he said a little less seriously. "First, forget everything you know about flying twin-engine aircraft."

I was surprised. "Why would we do that?" I asked.

"The Commander is different," Burns answered; his leg was going again. "It's easier to teach you how to fly it from scratch than to explain the differences and expect you to remember which is which."

"We read the aircraft manual," I countered. "We didn't see much different about it."

"I was afraid of that," Burns sighed. "There is very little accurate information in those 1950's manuals. Forget what you read."

I could feel my face turning red.

"We're listening," Henry said before I could boil over.

"Good. This airplane holds a maximum of 156 US gallons of fuel. We'll count on 148 being useable in level flight. The fuel burn will be 36 US gallons per hour giving us four hours and six minutes flying to fuel exhaustion."

He spoke quickly and quietly, and without referring to his binder. Henry and I made notes.

"With 45 minutes minimum reserve, we have three hours and 21 minutes flying time in visual conditions. With a block-to-block cruising speed of 160 knots at 6,000 feet, we get a range of 534 nautical miles in no wind."

"The book says it will do over 200 mph at 70 per cent power," I pointed out. "That's at least 175 knots."

"The book is wrong," Burns answered. His leg popped up and down. He continued, "The estimated empty weight is 4,400 pounds. The maximum allowable is 6,000 leaving 1,600 pounds useful load. You have to balance load and distance."

Ziggy's figures did not match anything I had read. I looked at Henry. He was avoiding eye contact with me as he scribbled with his head down.

"When you subtract 200 pounds for the pilot and his gear, and 50 pounds for oil, it leaves 462 pounds for passengers and baggage with full fuel. That's two medium-sized construction workers each carrying a toothbrush."

"We can fly that load in a Cherokee 140," I declared, dropping my pen on the table.

"True," Ziggy replied, "but only at 100 knots, in good weather and in a cabin that would require you to dismantle each construction worker before fitting them in."

He was right but it didn't help. "What's Petterson going to say when we tell him that he bought a two-passenger airplane?"

"Don't tell him. It isn't true," he replied. "For example, a trip to Sudbury from here will be one hour and 37 minutes in no wind. With an extra 45 minutes for VFR reserves, you'll need 505 pounds of fuel. That leaves weight for three construction workers and 55 pounds of cargo, or leave the cargo and carry more fuel to make North Bay an alternate in bad weather."

I couldn't calculate the math at his pace so I had to assume it was correct. I guess it bothered me because he sounded so sure of himself.

He saw my deepening frown. "Look," he said, leaning forward and pushing on his jumpy knee, "your customer bought an old airplane. He could have paid more for a fancier, newer one that flies higher and faster on less fuel but this machine is going to be a construction shuttle. The time and fuel difference on most trips will be small. Construction workers are never in a hurry anyway. The Commander is quiet, roomy and comfortable. They'll love it. They'll fall asleep as soon as they're airborne. The airplane is also one of the most stable platforms to fly. It will make you look like a good pilot. Give it a chance." He leaned back and sipped his coffee.

I looked at Henry. He was smiling but not talking. I could tell he liked this know-it-all little pilot. I decided there was no point butting heads.

"OK," I replied. "You have the floor."

"Thank you. There are only two times when you know exactly how much fuel is on board. There is a header tank above the baggage compartment connected to a bladder tank in the right wing. They both fill through the cap on top of the right wing. When the wing tank is full, they're both full. The cockpit fuel gauge only indicates the quantity in the header tank so it shows full until you burn off everything in the wing."

"What's the other time we know that the fuel quantity is accurate?" I asked.

Ziggy flashed his crooked smile. "When the engines quit," he said.

Henry chuckled. I shrugged. I deserved that one.

Ziggy continued. "Start with full fuel whenever deadheading solo and then log your flying time. The mixture is automatic so the fuel consumption is fixed for each power setting." He drank more coffee while Henry and I wrote notes.

"A quirk to remember when filling for full fuel is to wait ten minutes after it reaches the top of the wing tank and then fill it again. The fuel flows down to the header tank slower than you can pump it. Finish your walkaround and then go back. It should take six more gallons."

"Six gallons won't make much difference," I suggested.

Henry answered before Ziggy. "Six minutes," he replied.

Ziggy smiled again. "That's right; 16 more miles at cruise."

I nodded for him to continue.

"Now for balancing the load, start with one passenger aft, one forward, another aft and one in the middle."

"What about the other middle seat?" Henry asked.

"You can't carry five passengers unless they're children, so take it out. That frees up another 30 pounds for fuel or cargo and the construction workers will have more leg room or a place to store personal gear."

"How do we stay balanced during a training flight with two in the front?" I asked. I thought maybe I had bested him on this one.

"You carry a 25-pound sandbag in the baggage compartment but we won't need it today."

"Because we're not flying?" I suggested.

"No, because we'll fly two in the front and one in the back."

"The regulations say no passengers during training flights," I declared.

"That's correct," he answered patiently, "but your pilot licences qualify you to fly all airplanes in this weight category so we won't call it a training flight. With both of you on board, you'll learn twice as fast."

I realized that I was butting heads again.

When Ziggy saw that I wasn't challenging his answer, he said, "I brought you a 25-pound sandbag for trips when there is only one passenger and he wants to sit up front."

"Let me guess," Henry smiled, "it's in the right rear side of your Volkswagen."

"Yes, how did you know?"

"Your crooked car told me as you drove in."

Ziggy laughed for the first time that morning. So did I.

"Speaking of flying," Ziggy said, "let's take a break and start getting the airplane ready."

"The airplane is covered with ice," Henry said.

"I saw it walking in. That's why I suggest we start de-icing it."

"We don't have a de-icing truck," Henry explained.

"Do you have an engine pre-heater?" our instructor asked.

"Yes, we have two car warmers and a small propane heater with two hot air hoses."

"Good. We'll also need a short ladder, a couple of screwdrivers and some garden hose."

"But the airport is closed," I said.

Ziggy stood up. "We'll worry about that when we're ready to fly."

Henry and I exchanged puzzled looks.

Ziggy walked to the door and stopped with his hand on the knob. "One of you find the screwdrivers and cut two three-foot lengths of garden hose. The other can roll out the engine heater to the Commander."

He opened the door and was gone.

Henry and I did what we were told. When we had assembled everything in front of the airplane, Ziggy explained that we were going to de-ice the wings by opening inspection panels underneath and inserting the engine pre-heater hoses.

"Where the ice doesn't melt, we'll beat it off with the garden hose," he said.

We rigged the hot air tubes into the holes we opened under the left wing and then fired up the heater.

"Stick the car warmers on the pilot seats to heat up the instruments, radios and windshields," Ziggy said.

With that done, we headed back inside the office. Ziggy went straight to the coffeepot. "We'll finish the briefing," he said, "and then de-ice the other wing."

"I'll make fresh coffee," Henry offered.

"No need to waste this," Ziggy replied holding up the pot of thick black liquid. He poured it into his cup.

"Didn't you find it cold outside with no coat or socks?" I asked him.

"No, I never use them until mid-November," he said with a smile. "No sense wearing them out too soon."

This guy was either pulling my leg or he was the most painfully frugal person I had ever met. I looked out the window at the top of the Commander's wing. Water was already running from two spots above the heater hoses.

We sat down at the briefing table.

"This airplane will take off and land in less than 1,000 feet," Ziggy announced.

I didn't believe him. "At maximum weight?" I asked.

"That's correct. You don't normally need to operate from fields that short but it'll come in handy at construction sites."

"What about obstacles?" I asked. "There's no point horsing the airplane off the ground in less than 1,000 feet if it won't climb."

"No horsing required. Extend the flaps, hold the brakes, apply full power and let her go. Rotate at 85 mph and climb at 95 to clear obstacles."

"And snap the gear up after liftoff to help the climb?" I asked.

"No, the gear and flaps stay down until you reach 500 feet or clear any obstacles, whichever comes last."

"What if an engine fails?"

"Especially if an engine fails," Ziggy replied. "The hydraulic pump supplying pressure for the landing gear and flap retraction is on the left engine only. There is no sense unlocking the gear if it won't retract."

"But it's a twin-engine aircraft. Can't we just continue on one engine by retracting the gear and flap?"

"If either engine develops a problem after takeoff and below 500 feet, throttle back both engines and land on whatever is ahead."

"But why buy a twin if you can't keep going?"

"The few seconds it takes to climb above 500 feet on both engines is a small percentage of the flight time. Trust me, you can't gain altitude with this airplane on one engine. So from any altitude, the good engine will just take you to a better landing spot."

Ziggy was contradicting the Commander handbook and everything I knew about multi-engine flying, but then, he had said he would. I didn't ask any more questions. His hand had already enlarged the wear patch on his jumpy left knee.

"Don't land short unless you need to and then warn your passengers first. The brakes are large and effective. A maximum effort landing is likely to launch everyone into the cockpit."

Ziggy went on to describe how we should operate the engines. They had special floating counterweights on the crankshafts. The propellers were bolted to a gearbox that reduced the prop rotation speed to half that of the engine. This allowed more power from the engines and more efficiency from the props. Ziggy explained that this setup didn't catch on because the engines and transmissions scattered into expensive pieces when the pilots did not handle them properly.

"You don't want to be one of those pilots," he grinned.

Before breaking for lunch, we moved the propane heater to the other wing. The left one was clear of ice and dry except for the tips. The ice on the windshields was melting from the car warmers inside.

Back in the office, Ziggy pulled a thin, fowl-smelling sandwich from his binder along with a large bunch of grapes that was miraculously not squished.

"Help yourself," he said as he placed the grapes in the middle of the table. "I've been stealing these from the local vineyards since I read that the government is subsidizing the farmers to grown them for grape juice. Then the juice is dumped into sewers because of over-production."

We talked some more. I asked Ziggy about his limp.

"My left shoe was wearing faster than my right," he replied, "so I've been putting more weight on my right leg."

"Frugal" was no longer enough to describe how painfully cheap this pint-sized instructor was but it didn't matter. It was his Aero Commander experience that was important and he obviously had a lot of it.

Chapter Twenty

Ice dancing

We were in the Goose parked on the ice-covered ramp with both engines running. Henry was strapped into the left front seat and Ziggy was in the right. I was doing the work of a sandbag by sitting on the rear bench.

Ziggy reached for the microphone, "Circus Ground, Commander Charlie Gulf Oscar Oscar Sierra, ready to taxi, for circuits."

The overhead speaker barked to life. "Commander Charlie Gulf Oscar Oscar Sierra, Circus Ground, be advised that the Circus Airport is closed until further notice by NOTAM."

"How did you get to work?" Ziggy asked the controller.

"Say again, Oscar Oscar Sierra?"

"How did you get to the control tower if the airport is closed?"

There was a pause. "I drove in," the controller answered.

"But the airport is closed," Ziggy said.

"All the airport runways and taxiways are closed," the controller explained.

"The NOTAM doesn't say that," Ziggy countered. "The NOTAM closes the airport. To me, that includes the roads, your control tower and everything else."

"Stand... by..." the controller said slowly.

"While we're standing by," Ziggy continued, "we'll taxi out to the runway."

"I can't authorize that," the controller answered hastily.

"I know," Ziggy transmitted back, "the airport is closed, but you drove on the airport at your own discretion so we are taxiing out Delta Bravo for Runway 24 at our own discretion."

Ziggy nodded to Henry, "Go ahead slowly. When we're halfway across the ramp, try the brakes. You'll be surprised how much friction there is on clear ice."

Henry advanced the throttles. The sound of the engines increased slightly. It was hard to believe that an airplane that was so noisy outside could be so quiet in the cabin. I was sitting eight feet from the cockpit but I could hear the pilots' conversations.

Henry touched the brakes, the nose dipped and the airplane stopped.

"Don't count on that kind of braking for turning or stopping from high speed," Ziggy explained. "To turn onto the taxiway, apply right pedal to turn the rudder and nosewheel and then add power to the left engine."

Henry very gingerly did what he was told. The goose inched around the corner.

"You'll get the hang of it with practice," Ziggy said.

The controller's voice broke in, "Commander Charlie Gulf Oscar Oscar Sierra, this is Circus Ground."

"Go ahead," Ziggy replied.

"Be advised that the airport manager is issuing another NOTAM that will declare the Circus Airport runways, taxiways and ramps closed until further notice."

"Thank you," Ziggy said. "Until it comes out, we'll enjoy the nice weather and the unique conditions to do some circuits."

"I can't authorize that," the controller snapped back.

"That's right," Ziggy replied. Then to Henry, he said, "Park beside the runway. Use about 1,800 rpm for a run-up check. The brakes should hold."

Henry stopped the goose facing into the wind. He ran the power up to 1,800 rpm which gave a propeller speed of 900 rpm. The brakes held. He finished the rest of the pre-take-off checks.

"Backtrack to the button of Runway 24," Ziggy directed.

"Isn't Runway 28 closer to the wind?" Henry asked hopefully.

"Yes," Ziggy smiled, "that's why we're using 24, crosswind practice."

"On shear ice?"

"Yes. During the backtrack, try some medium speed turns to judge the nosewheel response."

Henry applied power. Ziggy announced our backtrack on the radio. The airplane trickled onto the runway. As Henry gained confidence, he allowed the speed to increase. Halfway to the beginning of the runway he got rolling too fast. The nosewheel started sliding. We were headed for the left side of the runway.

Ziggy made no attempt to take control. He sat calmly with his arms folded. "Turn with power. Bring the right throttle back and the left engine will turn us to the right."

It worked.

The heater wasn't delivering much warm air but Henry was sweating.

"Try the S-turns again," Ziggy said.

Henry soon had the big airplane sashaying down the runway in semi-control. My bum muscles tightened every time we slid.

"When you're in position to go," Ziggy instructed, "accelerate to 70 mph with full power and then abort the takeoff."

"Abort? Isn't that a little dangerous in these conditions?" Henry asked as he slowed the Goose to a stop at the button of Runway 24.

In the back, I nodded my head up and down vigorously in agreement.

"I'd rather practise the first half of the takeoff and the last part of the landing," Ziggy calmly explained, "than going airborne without knowing if we can land and stop."

Henry thought about it for a few moments. "I see your point but it still sounds dicey."

"Flying is managing risk," Ziggy added. "Go for the aborted takeoff."

"Whatever you say," Henry sighed. "With the wind from the right, the airplane will weathercock to the right. Should I use less power on the left engine?"

"That's correct, but only at the beginning of the roll. The rudder will be effective early. As it does, match up full power on both engines."

"Should I start on the left side of the runway so the crown will help keep us straight?" Henry asked. "I'll have more room to stop the swing to the right."

"Good suggestion but I favour the middle," Ziggy replied. "You have an equal chance of overcorrecting or undercorrecting."

"And how do I stop at the other end?"

"Idle power, full flaps and gentle brakes. If that doesn't work, then we'll turn the airplane around with differential power until we're sliding backward and then add power to both engines to stop."

Henry looked at him in disbelief. So did I.

"It shouldn't be necessary," Ziggy added.

I looked at the door handle beside me. I wanted to be sure that I knew how to open it so I could jump out before we slid into the boondocks.

Henry turned the airplane into position for takeoff. Ziggy announced our intentions on the radio. Henry added power. It wasn't long before positive rudder control allowed him to move the throttles all the way forward. Seventy mph came quickly. Henry cut the power and applied brakes. The tire out my left window stop rotating. The Commander slid down the runway and began turning into the wind.

"More left rudder," Ziggy commanded. His voice was clear and calm. His arms remained folded across his chest. "Ease off the brakes. You have to be your own anti-skid control. Now add power on the right engine to keep straight."

The Goose slalomed down the runway as Henry searched for the right

If Clouds Could Talk

The nosewheel started sliding. We were headed for the side of the runway.

amount of corrections. Each swing of the tail was magnified in the back seat. I felt like I was in a game of "Crack-the-whip."

Eventually Henry tamed the Goose without going into the grass. He stopped us before the end of the runway.

"Swing the airplane around," Ziggy said. "We'll let your partner have a go." He turned his head in my direction. "It's your turn," he said.

A lump rose in my throat. I unfastened my seat belt.

"Good luck," Henry said to me as we passed mid-cabin.

"Thanks, slider," I replied.

Ziggy briefed me as I strapped into the pilot seat. "Start by doing S-turns to the other end. Control with nosewheel, rudder and alternate engine power but not too much of each."

I added 100 rpm to both engines. The Goose barely moved.

"You're doing fine," Ziggy said, "except it'll be dark before we get there. Pick up the pace."

I applied more power. It felt like I was driving an elephant wearing skates. Eventually I gained confidence and managed to snake the Goose to the other end of the runway and turn it around.

"Try the aborted takeoff," Ziggy said. "Accelerate to 70 mph and then stop."

I applied full throttle on the right engine and a little less on the left. The Goose accelerated rapidly. Control became easy as the speed increased.

Ziggy's knee started jiggling when I accidentally blasted through 70 to 80 mph before cutting the power. I extended full flap and braked. The wheels locked. The airplane slid. I released some pedal pressure. The airplane slowed but that transferred more weight to the nosewheel. It steered like a loaded wheelbarrow down a hill.

"Control wheel full back!" Ziggy barked.

I pulled but the Goose had already commenced an almighty swing into the wind.

"Let it go around!" Ziggy commanded. His voice was rising and his knee was bouncing madly. "Lock the left brake so it slides. Add full right rudder."

I stepped on the top of the left pedal while pushing the right pedal all the way in. The airplane rotated to the right while sliding sideways toward the end of the runway.

"Release left brake. Add power on the right," he ordered, "lots of power!"

I did as he said. The rotation slowed as we reached the half-turn point.

"Power up on the left. Squeeze both brakes."

We were now sliding backward at a good clip. Ziggy's arms were no longer folded. His left hand was pressed hard on his jumpy knee. His right hand was pointing to his next command. The Goose was still turning gently to the right. "More power on the right," Ziggy called out. "Now more power on both."

The airplane stopped rotating and slowed its backward slide. The numbers "06" rolled out from under the blue nose. We stopped.

My hands and feet stayed locked on the controls.

"Power to idle," Ziggy instructed.

His pumping leg settled down. I forced myself to relax my grip.

"Switch seats with Henry before that new NOTAM comes into effect," Ziggy said. "I'll hold the brakes."

I unbuckled and climbed out of my seat. I was hot, clammy and angry. I couldn't see the point in placing the Goose at risk just to practise dancing on an ice-covered runway, something that would never be done in corporate flying.

"Good luck," I said passing Henry in the cabin.

"Yeah, thanks."

The cabin speaker came alive. "Commander Golf Oscar Oscar Sierra, Circus Ground. A revised NOTAM is coming through now."

Ziggy waved Henry into the pilot seat. He left the microphone on the hook.

"Golf Oscar Oscar Sierra, do you read?"

Ziggy waited for Henry to fasten his seat belts before replying.

"This is Oscar Oscar Sierra, go ahead."

"A new NOTAM for the Circus Airport, effective five minutes ago: 'All runways, taxiways and ramps closed until further notice.' What are your intentions?"

"Oscar Oscar Sierra will exit the Circus Airport manoeuvring areas immediately," Ziggy announced.

I had no idea what our instructor had in mind but I was sure I wouldn't like it.

Ziggy turned to Henry, "You use the north side of this runway for grass field practice, don't you?"

"Yes," my partner answered with some hesitation.

"Taxi over there and backtrack for a soft-field takeoff."

"The grass is crusted with ice," Henry protested. "We'll chew up the props and get stuck."

"Not if you keep us moving. Hit the grass with lots of power on, be ready to take off when we turn around at the other end and don't depart in our previous track."

Henry took a hard, questioning look at Ziggy.

Ziggy returned the stare and said, "I know what I'm doing."

Henry powered the Goose into the grass, pulled the control wheel back to lever some weight off the nosewheel and retracted the flaps so they would not be damaged by ice from the tires.

Ziggy spoke calmly into the microphone. "Oscar Oscar Sierra is back-tracking the grass north of Runway 24 for a grass departure and a local flight west."

After a pause the controller responded. "I can't authorize that, Oscar Oscar Sierra."

"That's correct," Ziggy replied, "but your airspace is open so how about giving us the wind and altimeter setting."

There was another pause. "Altimeter 30.08, wind 300 degrees at 15 gusting to 18. No reported traffic."

"Roger, thank you, Oscar Oscar Sierra."

The Commander rolled through the glazed turf surprising well. The big main wheels broke the crust into chunks, which were blown back by the propellers, but I couldn't hear anything hitting the fuselage.

"Use lots of right engine power to swing us around and then keep going with both throttles to the wall," Ziggy instructed, "and don't forget the crosswind."

He punched the microphone button. "Oscar Oscar Sierra departing the grass at Circus for a local flight west."

Henry powered the big twin around, lined up parallel to our taxi tracks, slowly applied full power, fed in some aileron to the right and extended the flaps. The engines revved to 3,600 rpm. The Goose eagerly galloped ahead. Soon the nose came up. Henry held it until the airplane pulled itself free of the surface.

Inside the cabin, the sound of the big Lycoming engines at full song was sweet. The bark of the straight-through exhaust was left behind. I was hearing the muted pulse of twelve cylinders beating out their powerful strokes and the steady zing of the propellers cutting the air at 1,800 rpm.

"Nose down to build speed," Ziggy said. I could hear him clearly. "Full flaps until you establish a climb. Full throttle remains for the climb to prevent the automatic mixture from leaning. Level off at four thousand five hundred feet."

We flew for two hours. Henry and I exchanged seats several times. Ziggy had us doing turns, stalls and slow flight. He frequently pulled the mixture on one engine or the other to simulate an engine failure. At altitude, he proved that the Goose would not climb on one engine in an over-shoot configuration. He had us test all of the cockpit equipment. Every-thing worked except the Number 2 VOR navigation receiver.

We flew westward to the Derry Airport. I was in the pilot seat when Ziggy produced a set of eyeglass frames with a cardboard hood taped over the top.

"Try these on," he said handing them to me.

His homemade instrument simulator was very effective. I could not see outside except for the odd glimpse of ground in the corner of the big windshield.

Then Ziggy placed some photocopied IFR approach charts to Derry's runways in my lap. He worked the radios while directing me to practise flying the approaches. The simulated engine cuts continued. My legs grew sore from holding the airplane on course with rudder on one engine.

"Use aileron to help fly straight," Ziggy suggested.

It worked.

He was a hard man to warm up to but he was gaining my respect. There didn't seem to be anything that he didn't know.

The runways at Derry had been treated with urea, a non-salt, ice melter. They were damp but not slippery. We practised stop and go landings and takeoffs at the end of each instrument approach.

I was flying with the hooded eyeglass frames when we returned to the Circus Control Zone.

"Circus Tower, Commander Gulf Oscar Oscar Sierra, ten west at 3,500, request a simulated NDB approach to Runway 06."

"Commander Gulf Oscar Oscar Sierra, Circus Tower, simulated NDB approach approved, winds 280 at 15, altimeter 30.10. Call by the Circus Beacon outbound."

"Oscar Oscar Sierra."

"Set up an NDB approach," Ziggy said to me. "When you reach circling minimums, take the hood off."

"OK. I'm descending now," I replied. I reduced the power.

"Oscar Oscar Sierra, Circus Tower."

"Go ahead," Ziggy answered.

"Oscar Oscar Sierra be advised that Runway 06/24 and taxiway Bravo have been sanded on their 50-foot centres. A revised NOTAM is in effect opening them for aircraft manoeuvring at the pilot's discretion."

"Roger, Oscar Sierra."

I couldn't believe it. Barney, the skinflint airport manager, had purchased hot sand for the main runway and taxiway. Ziggy's actions must have goaded him into it.

The ADF needle became lively, indicating we were close to the beacon four miles off the end of Runway 06. When it swung to point behind us, I turned the Goose away from the airport and told Ziggy that I was by the beacon outbound.

"Oscar Sierra is by the Circus Beacon outbound," he announced on the radio.

"Oscar Sierra, roger. What are your intentions following this approach?"

"We will be landing at Circus, tower."

"Roger Oscar Sierra, will you be landing on Runway 24?"

"Negative," Ziggy replied. "We don't want to sandblast our airplane. We'll be circling for a landing in the grass on the north side of Runway 24."

There was a long pause before the controller answered, "Roger, Oscar Sierra, call by the beacon inbound."

"Oscar Sierra."

I turned right for a 45-degree intercept of the inbound track to the airport. When I was on it, I completed a pre-landing check, lowering the landing gear and flaps.

I knew our grass landing would be a slap in the wallet for Barney. I decided when we got back to the office, I would not answer the phone for the rest of the day.

The ADF needle wiggled and flipped.

"By the beacon inbound," I called to Ziggy.

"Oscar Sierra is by the Circus Beacon inbound," he said into the microphone.

"Oscar Sierra, roger, you are cleared for a circling approach. Land in the grass at your own discretion, wind 290 at 13."

"Oscar Sierra.

"Set up for a soft-field landing to the right of where Henry took off," Ziggy said.

"OK, coach," I replied.

"Oscar Sierra," the controller said, "the airport manager reports the braking on the sanded parts of the airport to be fair to good."

"Thank you, tower. I'll remember that next time I'm driving a dump truck on the runway. We'll land in the grass."

"Roger, land at your own discretion, wind 290 at 10."

I imagined that Barney would be spitting nails after hearing that comment but it was fun to hear Ziggy show some humour.

"Be ready with the power to keep us moving after touchdown," the little pilot said to me.

"Yes, sir."

I descended to 600 feet above the ground, leveled off, removed the hood and declared the airport in sight.

"After landing, taxi to the runway but stay out of the sand."

I sensed that my instructor was nervous about something. From the corner of my eye, I could see his left leg jiggling up and down again. He pushed on it with his left hand.

I considered messing up a little by porpoising the Goose to give Ziggy something to worry about. I decided against it when I realized that the tailwind had pushed the big twin along. I was now falling behind the approach. I slowed the Goose and caught up to her. Ziggy's leg stopped jumping. He had known that I was behind before I had.

On final, everything looked good. I flared out and held the Goose off the grass until the nose was higher than I thought it would go.

"Any danger of hitting the tail, Ziggy?" I asked quickly.

Before he could answer, the airplane plopped onto the crunchy grass and slowed without braking. I turned left toward the edge of the runway and added power.

"No," Ziggy said.

"No what?" I asked in surprise.

"There's no danger of hitting the tail."

"Thanks."

"Circus Tower, Oscar Sierra requests taxi clearance to the ramp."

"Taxi at your own discretion, Oscar Sierra. Be advised that only the centre 50-feet of the runway and taxiway are sanded."

"Oscar Sierra."

Ziggy turned to me. "Do you suppose the airport manager would bring the sweeper out to clear the sand where we cross the runway?"

"He'd freak," I said without hesitation.

"OK, backtrack to the intersection, build up some speed and then coast across."

"Are runway contaminants that hard on this airplane?" I asked.

"Yes, it's low slung. That's why the propeller blades are new and the paint is beat up. The former owner has been operating into gravel strips."

I stopped talking and concentrated on negotiating along the narrow band of ice-covered asphalt between the sand and the runway edge. I coasted across the sand to get to the taxiway and turned carefully onto The Flying Circus ramp.

While I was going through the shut-down check, Ziggy pulled out the aircraft logbook and made an entry. I decided that I was warming up to his combination of knowledge, confidence and dry sense of humour.

"That was great, Ziggy," I said. "I don't know where Darcy found you, but I'm glad he did."

Henry came forward and stuck his head between our seats, "Yes, thank you very much," he said. "You sure know how to make a Commander dance."

"You're welcome," Ziggy replied. "You two should be fine now. Try some solo practice before carrying passengers." He patted the glareshield on top of the instrument panel and said, "The airplane seems to be in good shape. She looks rough but everything works except that Number 2 VOR indicator."

The three of us were smiling as we stepped out of the airplane and slid our way across the ramp to the office. Inside, Ziggy gathered up his old binder.

Henry wrote a cheque to cover his pay. I made idle chatter. "I thought there were only a few of this type of Commander in the country. Where did you fly one?" I asked.

Ziggy frowned. He accepted the cheque from Henry, read it and stuffed it into his shirt pocket. "Who said I had?" he replied. "I've never been in an Aero Commander before."

The little man walked to the door, opened it and said, "Good bye."

We watched him negotiate the slippery sidewalk. He was favouring his left shoe.

I looked at my partner. "Is my mouth hung open like yours?"

Henry looked at me. "Yes."

Chapter Twenty-one

Some days...

Itelephoned Darcy the next day. "You said Ziggy Burns was an Aero Commander expert."

"Good morning to you too," the mechanic replied. "What's the problem?"

"The man had never flown a Commander before!"

"That's correct. He told me that he had never even been in one."

"Yeah, that's my point," I pretended to grumble.

"Well, I told you that I knew someone who could check you out. Was I wrong?"

"Where did you find this guy?"

"He's been around. You didn't answer my question."

"Ziggy was great. He knew all kinds of stuff about the airplane. I've never learned so much so quickly from someone so small," I laughed. "And then the squirt tells me it's his first flight in the airplane."

"He usually doesn't mention that detail. It upsets some people."

"I asked him straight out."

"Serves you right."

"Where did he learn so much?"

"He pays attention, uses his head and remembers."

"Is he a pilot?"

"If he is," Darcy chuckled, "he's the first with those qualifications."

"Smart guy. So you don't know if he has a pilot licence or not?"

"No I don't. I never asked him. Did you?"

"Ah... no."

"Is that why you called?"

"No. The Commander's Number 2 VOR indicator stopped working."

"How do you know it's the indicator?"

"Because Ziggy said it was."

"OK. The radio guys can look at it Thursday morning. Bring two pilots and one can fly your Cherokee back."

"Thank you."

"You're welcome.

Thursday was my day off. I told Henry about getting the VOR indicator fixed that day. He said, "I'll take care of it, you take your day off."

We both needed to practise flying the big twin. Henry's tone told me that he was counting on me volunteering to go with him. He knew I'd feel guilty.

"I'll fly with you Thursday but we have to leave early and I get to fly the Commander back."

"But it's your day off," Henry smiled.

"It is, but if I don't go, I'll feel guilty. If I sacrifice half a day, then you'll feel guilty and I still might accomplish something at home."

"You're on," he laughed.

"We'll fly there and have coffee. If they can't find the problem right away, we'll leave the unit and fly both airplanes home."

"Aye, aye captain!"

On Wednesday afternoon, a large warm front moved into the Circus area. The forecast called for two days of low clouds and rain. Henry and I arranged to meet in the weather office at eight o'clock the next morning.

At first light, the clouds were hanging low and it was drizzling. I drove to the airport and parked my Volkswagen behind Henry's Pinto outside the Circus Terminal. The weather office was in a trailer attached to one end of the small building.

Inside, Henry was studying the met maps clipped to the wall. Sonny Paleman, the weatherman, was preparing his eight o'clock report for the Circus Airport.

"Good morning," Henry said. "Sonny's calling the cloud base at 200 feet and the visibility half a mile in fog. The forecast predicts improvement this morning. To the west, Windsor already has 3,000 feet and 10 miles."

"Are you guys going on the same trip?" Sonny asked.

"We are," I replied.

Sonny was a nervous, middle-aged homebody who did everything by the book. He had never been flying, a situation he vowed to maintain.

"Won't The Flying Circus be wiped out if you crash?" he asked.

"It might," I replied, "but half-baked pilots like us are twice as likely to crash if we fly solo. Flying together is the lesser of two evils."

"Makes sense to me," he replied, "but it's not very far to Derry."

"Yes, but we're flying that new airplane," I added. "It's very complex. It really takes two pilots just to get it off the ground."

Sonny looked to see if I was pulling his leg. I kept a straight face and goaded him further. "We don't have any passengers today. How about coming for the ride?"

The weatherman held up his hand as if to ward me off. "Not me. Besides you can't go, the weather is below minimums."

"But the forecast says it will lift soon," Henry said.

"That's what it says."

Airports have published weather minimums for taking off and landing in bad weather. At Circus it was 300 feet and one mile visibility for departure and 600 feet and one mile for arrival.

We checked the reports from the weather offices west of Circus as they came in. They all showed improvement except Derry which was built on higher ground.

We left Sonny and drove over to The Flying Circus. Henry filed a flight plan for a nine o'clock departure to Derry with Kitchener as an alternate. I did the pre-flight inspection in the drizzle. Then Henry came out and helped me pull the Goose to the fuel pump.

"Better fill it up," Henry said. "Then we know exactly how much we have and we're covered if the weather forecast is wrong."

"Aye, aye captain."

I dragged the hose and the ladder to the right wing. Henry stepped into the airplane to ready the cockpit for our departure.

Full fuel gave us four hours flying time at cruise. We could throttle back and fly longer if we needed. Our plan was for Henry to fly to Derry as pilot-in-command. I would monitor how he was doing, throw him a few curves and intervene only if he got behind what was going on.

At 8:40, Henry started both engines and called for taxi instructions. The ground controller gave us clearance to Runway 24. I saw Sonny step out of the weather office with a balloon. I watched as he released it and timed its ascent into the clouds.

Henry stopped the Goose beside the runway. The controller called in a few minutes and said that Sonny's special weather observation was 200 feet and one mile.

I answered. "We'll wait here for the next report if that's OK."

"No problem," the controller replied.

Henry nodded in agreement and shut the engines down on the taxiway. We left one communication radio turned on.

We passed the time reviewing rejected takeoffs, engine failures after lift-off, landing gear malfunctions and run-a-way propellers.

Sonny emerged from his trailer with his stopwatch and another heli-

"You want to measure the height of the cloud above the ground? Well, this is the ground."

um-filled balloon a few minutes before nine o'clock.

"I'll help him this time," I said to Henry. I bolted from my seat, opened the cabin door and hotfooted toward Sonny.

"Hey!" I yelled, "I'll give you a hand."

The weatherman turned his head my way and frowned. "I don't need help."

"Well," I said as I drew up beside him, "I watched you during your last report. You released the balloon and then started the watch. To be accurate, they should be done together."

His frown deepened but he hesitated. I reached for the balloon.

"Here, I'll let the balloon go the instant you hit the button on the watch."

149

"Well, OK," he replied reluctantly.

I knelt down and held the balloon against the ground.

"What are you doing?"

"You want to measure the height of the cloud above the ground, don't you? Well, this is the ground."

"I don't think that'll make any difference," he said.

"I'm ready when you are," I replied.

I watched his hand. He thumbed the button. "Now!"

I held the balloon until I saw his eyes move down from the watch toward the ground, then I let it go.

"Perfect!" I declared.

Sonny frowned some more but kept his eyes on the balloon. The red rubber ball rose rapidly. It soon became a dot. I watched Sonny. When I saw his hand tighten on the stopwatch, I declared, "I can still see it!"

"You can?"

"Yes... still... oh, now it's gone!"

I looked down at Sonny. He was thumbing the "stop" button. He read the numbers. "The ceiling must have gone up a bit," he said.

"OK thanks," I replied. "I'll get your full report from the tower. Are you sure you can't come with us?"

"Positive. Somebody has to stay alive to monitor the weather."

"And we're glad you do!"

I trotted back to the airplane. I had no idea if I had stretched Sonny's timing to give us a departure-limits ceiling, but it was worth a try.

By the time I had regained my seat, the tower controller called with the nine o'clock weather reports for our trip. At Circus, the ceiling was now 300 feet and the visibility was one mile. We had our take-off minimums. Derry was still reporting 100 feet and a quarter mile. Kitchener was holding at 500 feet and one mile, good enough for an alternate.

"When you want to go," the controller said, "I'll request your clearance from Toronto Centre."

"We'll go now, " Henry answered.

He started the engines and completed the pre-take-off check. The controller came back with our clearance for an instrument flight to Derry. Henry copied it onto his kneepad and then read it back.

"Clearance correct," the controller said. "Taxi into position Runway 24 and standby for radar release."

"Oscar Sierra," Henry replied. He taxied the big Goose to the beginning of the runway and swung it around. The time was 09:15.

"Cleared for takeoff, Oscar Oscar Sierra. The wind is 220 at five. Sonny requests a ceiling check if you can."

"Oscar Sierra."

"I'll watch for the cloud base," I said to Henry.

"Roger."

He held the brakes with his toes, eased the power levers up, checked the engine instruments and then released. The acceleration pressed us into our seats. Henry divided his scanning time between the runway ahead and the flight instruments. I watched the engine instruments and what Henry was doing.

At 80 mph, Henry eased back on the control wheel. The nose of the Goose started to rise. He relaxed some back pressure. The airplane continued along the runway on its main wheels momentarily and then lifted off. Henry adjusted the nose up attitude to nail the climb speed at 95 mph. We started to encounter a few wisps of cloud at 200 feet above the ground. At 250 feet, we were in cloud more than out. By 300 feet, the ground had disappeared.

"The ceiling is 300 feet," I said into the microphone.

"Thank you Oscar Oscar Sierra. Over to Toronto Centre now on 133.3."

I should have said 250 feet but I wanted to convince Sonny that my helpful method of balloon timing was accurate.

Henry continued climbing in solid cloud to 4,000 feet and leveled off with a low power setting. He told Toronto Centre that we wanted to practise instrument approaches at Derry starting with a hold at the Stelco Fix. The traffic in our sector was light. The radar controller replied right away with a holding clearance. Henry read it back and set up for a parallel entry to a non-standard hold.

I tuned the Derry Automated Terminal Information Service frequency on my radio. The recording announced a ceiling at 100 feet and visibility of a quarter mile. The forecast had indicated that the cloud bases should be 600 feet by now.

Henry flew the entry plus once around hold and then asked for an approach clearance for a low and over on Runway 24.

"Oscar Oscar Sierra is cleared to the Derry Airport, Backcourse Localizer approach to Runway 24," the controller replied. "Call by the fix outbound."

"Oscar Sierra coming up to the fix outbound now," Henry replied.

"Roger, contact Derry Tower."

"Oscar Oscar Sierra.

"Derry, Oscar Oscar Sierra is with you by the Stelco Fix outbound descending to 2,800 feet."

"Call by fix inbound, Oscar Oscar Sierra and go ahead your intentions following the overshoot."

"Oscar Sierra requests a landing off the ILS approach to Runway 06."

"On the overshoot, ATC clears Oscar Oscar Sierra to the Derry Airport for the ILS approach to Runway 06."

Henry read the clearance back while intercepting the centreline for Runway 24. He lowered the landing gear and flaps, and descended.

"Oscar Sierra by the Stelco Fix inbound," Henry announced.

"Call on the missed approach, Oscar Oscar Sierra," the controller replied.

"Oscar Sierra."

Henry kept the localizer needle within two dots of centre. He leveled off at 400 feet, the minimum approach height for that runway. I peered ahead and down but could not see the ground or the runway.

Henry initiated an overshoot when his approach time had elapsed. "Oscar Sierra on the missed approach."

"Oscar Oscar Sierra, we check. Call by the Derry Beacon outbound."

"Oscar Sierra."

The minimum approach height for Runway 06 was 200 feet. If we didn't see the runway on this approach, our practice flight would become more challenging. The day-off part of my day off would be shorter.

Henry leveled the Goose at 2,000 feet. I pulled out the approach charts for Kitchener and studied them.

"Oscar Sierra Derry Beacon outbound," Henry announced into the microphone.

"Call by the beacon inbound, Oscar Oscar Sierra, and I have a special weather observation for Derry when you're ready to copy."

I signaled to Henry that I would get it. "Oscar Sierra is ready to copy now," I said.

"Derry special at 13:50 Zulu, 100 overcast and one half mile in fog..."

"Thank you. Can you get the latest Kitchener weather for us?" I asked.

"Roger, Kitchener at 13:00 Zulu, 500 overcast, visibility one mile in fog and light drizzle..."

"Oscar Sierra."

Henry entered a procedure turn to line up with the runway. He intercepted the localizer. The glideslope needle came alive. Henry extended the gear and flaps, and followed the glidepath down.

He nailed the approach. The ILS indicators were centred all the way to the 200-foot minimum altitude. The runway should have been in front of us. I could only see drizzle and mist.

"Nothing here," I barked.

Henry applied full power.

"On to Kitchener for more practice?" I suggested when we were established in the climb.

"Affirmative."

"Your approach was very good," I added.

"Thank you."

"I'll see if I can mess up the next one for you."

"Thank you, I think."

Henry advised the control tower on the overshoot and asked for a clearance to Kitchener. We were switched to Toronto Centre. The radar controller gave us our clearance. The time was 10:15.

We weren't worried about the weather. Kitchener was only 25 miles away and we had enough fuel to try a large number of the airports in the area if necessary.

A special weather report for Kitchener was passed to us indicating the ceiling was up to 800 feet with two miles visibility. Henry and I decided to practise two approaches there, land, switch seats and practise some more until Derry improved.

My partner was in a groove. I simulated a failure of the right engine on the first approach. His left leg was working hard to counteract the off-centre thrust of the left engine but we broke out of the cloud lined up with the runway. I restored the power to the right engine. Henry initiated an overshoot.

Seeing the ground took some pressure off our extended practice flight.

"Now I know why Ziggy was always exercising his left leg up and down," Henry joked.

I smiled, "That was only when I was bugging him."

"Yeah, which sounded like all the time to me," he laughed.

On the next approach I simulated a left engine failure. This meant the hydraulic pump on that engine was inoperative. Henry had to approach without extending the landing gear or flaps. I also covered his heading indicator with a stick-on soap dish to simulate its failure. He came in fast, maintaining headings by timing his turns and checking the compass when level. He was right on.

"Do you want an emergency gear extension," Henry asked, "or do you want me to belly in?"

I reached over and selected landing gear down. "Consider an emergency extension complete," I answered.

Henry flew to a full-stop landing and turned onto a taxiway. It was 11:30.

I asked the Kitchener Ground Controller for the latest Derry weather.

"Roger Oscar Oscar Sierra, Derry at 15:00 Zulu, 100 overcast, one half mile in drizzle and fog..."

"Thank you."

"Let's go to the ramp and gas up," Henry said.

"And find some coffee," I added.

We parked the Goose in front of the fuel pumps. No one came out so we walked in. A clean-cut young fellow greeted us from behind the desk.

"Looking for fuel?" he asked.

"Affirmative," Henry replied.

"We don't have any."

"You're out of 100 octane?" I was surprised.

"That's right. Been out four days but it's on order. Should come tomorrow. I guess you didn't see the Notice to Airmen," he added.

Henry blushed. He could have asked for notices affecting our flight from the specialist who took his flight plan.

"We didn't intend to come here," he said quietly.

"The coffee shop is open," the youngster offered.

"The engines don't run on coffee," I replied.

The kid didn't respond to my sarcasm.

"No, but I do," Henry said.

We had coffee. Then I phoned for the twelve o'clock weather reports and told Henry the news.

"It has improved a bit here and at home but Derry remains at 100 and half a mile," I said. "Why don't we have lunch, get ready to go and check again?"

"OK," he replied, then he smiled. "How much money do you have?"

I had the company credit card for fuel but I hadn't thought of cash. I checked my wallet and pockets.

"Five dollars and thirty-five cents," I said, slapping the money on the counter.

"Leanne gave me ten dollars emergency money."

"Let me guess; you're not supposed to spend it."

"I think lunch is an emergency, don't you?"

"Absolutely."

We each had the soup and sandwich special. With coffee, the bill came to eight dollars and ninety cents. We left a 45-cent tip.

"Ziggy would have been proud of our restraint on that tip," I whispered as we walked away.

Henry laughed. "I doubt it. We were forty cents too high."

We split the walkaround inspection. The fuel gauge indicated that the fuselage tank was still full but there was no way to tell how much remained in the wing tank. I borrowed the fuel ladder and climbed up to see if there was gas showing. There was.

We had flown two hours and 20 minutes. That left one hour and forty minutes of fuel at normal cruise speed but we had been flying slower. We decided to assume we had two hours of fuel remaining.

It was my turn to fly so I checked the one o'clock weather. The clouds at Kitchener were broken with bases at 800 feet. Circus reported 600 broken and six miles visibility. Derry had improved slightly to 200 feet overcast and three quarters of a mile visibility.

"Let's file a flight plan to Derry. If we don't get in, we'll go to Circus as our alternate. We need 45 minutes to fly to Derry and shoot two approaches. If we miss, it's on to Circus. That will take a half an hour including the approach leaving us with 45 minutes of reserve fuel if we miss at Circus."

"Sounds good to me," Henry replied.

We departed at one thirty and flew in cloud to Derry. I asked for and received radar vectors from Toronto Centre to intercept the straight-in backcourse approach to Runway 24. I captured the localizer and stayed on it during the descent. Henry did nothing to mess me up. At the 400-foot minimum height we were still in the cloud.

"Nothing," Henry declared when the approach time expired.

On the overshoot, I received a clearance for the ILS approach to Runway 06 at Derry. I flew that one, also without failures simulated by Henry. He wanted me to make the approach.

On final, I had the needles centered or close most of the time. The clouds in front of the windshield darkened as we neared the 200-foot minimum height. This was a sure sign of being close to the base of the cloud. I began to catch glimpses of the ground in my scan of the instrument panel and the windshield. Then the approach lights appeared, first one, then two and three at a time. My eyes followed them to the strobe lights at the runway threshold. I was ready to pull the power off and raise the nose for a landing. I saw the markings on the beginning of the runway.

"Go around!" Henry said loudly.

I hesitated, then I saw why. He had been looking ahead while I had been looking down. Without the lights and the heavy white paint markings, there was no runway. The clouds had thinned but in spots they continued to the ground. It would have been difficult to keep the Goose straight on the runway in such poor visibility.

I applied full power and raised the nose.

"That was a real sucker hole," Henry said.

"Now what?" I asked as we climbed out.

"On to Circus," he replied.

It was two fifteen. We had one hour and fifteen minutes fuel remaining. It was no longer a practice flight.

During the climbout to 3,000 feet, we broke into the sunshine above thinning cloud. On the way to Circus, we could see the ground in several places. The centre radar controller read the latest Circus weather to us. "Indefinite ceiling 100 feet, visibility zero in fog..."

I couldn't believe it. "Sonny must be joking or hallucinating," I said to Henry.

"I don't think he's capable of either but I'll double check."

He asked the controller to confirm the weather report was for Circus. It was, yet we could see the ground more and more as we flew eastward.

"Let's shoot an approach and see what's going on," I said to Henry.

"Okay. I'll check the weather at other airports."

My request for a straight in ADF approach to Runway 06 at the Circus Airport was granted. I lined up with the Circus non-directional beacon so that Runway 06 would be straight ahead on the other side of the city. As we flew closer, I could see the City of Circus sitting in wide-open sunshine. I descended and peered ahead. There was a streamer of fog off Lake Ontario blanketing the airport.

I called Circus Tower as we crossed over the beacon inbound. Barry McDay was working the afternoon shift. "Roger, Oscar Sierra, call with the runway in sight but from here it doesn't look good."

I descended to the minimum approach altitude of 600 feet. The top of the fog ahead was still below us.

"What's your visibility, Barry?" I asked on the tower frequency.

"Zero," Barry replied. "I can't see the ground from three floors up in the tower."

The time was two forty-five. We had 45 minutes of fuel remaining.

I looked at Henry. "OK partner, what's Plan C or E or whatever we're on?"

"Niagara Falls is open."

The Niagara Airport was only 12 miles away but it was in the United States. At this point, our priority was getting the airplane on the ground.

"Niagara Falls it is," I replied.

Halfway there we could see that the American airport was in the clear. Henry cancelled our IFR flight and I flew visually to a landing.

Niagara operated as a joint military and civil airport. It was home to the New York Air National Guard. It was also designated an airport of entry for international flights clearing into the United States. There were no airline flights so the customs staff drove from one of the nearby international bridges on request. By the book, customs required two hours notice before an aircraft landed for an inspection.

The Niagara Tower controller called the customs office for us. We landed and taxied to the ramp. There was no answer on the parking frequency so I picked a spot near the terminal building and shut down.

What looked like a 24-star army general came out and told us we couldn't park there. He pointed to a more acceptable spot 100 feet away. We moved.

The uniform worked for the Niagara Frontier Transportation Authority. The stars were long service pins. The man wanted a five-dollar landing fee.

We asked about fuel. He was in charge of that too. He would accept Exxon, Sohio, Philips or cash; but not Visa, which, with our Canadian six dollars, was all we had.

Before we could negotiate further, a pudgy but happy-looking U.S.

customs officer arrived. "Weather caught you out, did it boys?"

"Yes sir," Henry replied respectfully.

"There are two things you can always count on," he continued: "the weather forecast being wrong and some sucker flying anyway." He slapped his leg, bent over and laughed at his own joke.

I didn't think it was funny.

"Yes sir," Henry replied.

"Well, come on in and we'll fix you up."

He led us into the depths of the terminal building and sat us down in a small office.

"You fill in form Number 178(7-27-76) for your customs declarations," he said pushing a long piece of paper toward me. "And you can fill in Number 1-92A(REV.)3-1o-77y for immigration," he said to Henry.

"I'll take your birth certificates and run them through the computer."

Smiley wasn't in a hurry. We were done our paperwork before he finished checking our names through the electronic files.

When he was done, he asked, "Do you have a U.S. Customs User Decal for that airplane?"

"No sir," Henry replied.

"OK. There'll be a twenty-five dollar user decal fee and a twenty-five dollar overtime charge, cash in U.S. dollars."

"Why the overtime charge?" I asked politely.

"Because," he said, still grinning, "airport call-outs require a minimum of four man-hours. We officially close at five o'clock, so any call-out after one o'clock is overtime."

"So now you have to wait here for four hours?"

"Three. We count travel time."

"We don't have twenty-five American dollars," Henry said.

"No problem," Smiley replied. "You can charge the overtime by filling in this, form Number 1013."

Then he turned to me. "While he's doing that, you can complete form Number 5106. That rebates part of the twenty-five dollar overtime charge in the event that another aircraft lands for customs during the next three hours. Whoever finishes first can complete form number 503225, the User Fee Decal Request."

We finished clearing customs at ten minutes to four. The ramp general hailed us from down the hallway. "The tower has a message for you," he said. "You can use this phone."

The message was from Barry. The fog had dissipated. Circus Airport was clear.

The star-studded airport employee agreed to part with 10 gallons of fuel and cover his landing fee in exchange for a personal cheque. That assured us of at least 20 minutes of fuel for the 15-minute hop home.

"It's your turn to fly," I said to Henry. "I don't want a double engine failure on my shift. You check over the Goose. I'll file an international flight plan and advise Canada Customs."

"OK."

We could see the Circus Airport not long after we lifted off the runway at Niagara. Henry continued climbing until we were within gliding distance of Circus. He radioed Barry and was given a left base to Runway 24. We landed at four forty-five but our trip wasn't over.

Henry taxied to the terminal ramp and shut down the engines. We had to wait for a Canada Customs officer to drive from the same international bridge as the American agent.

A lady arrived. I let Henry explain why we claimed to have been out of the country for less than an hour. She looked in the empty airplane and let us go. It was five o'clock.

We taxied over to The Flying Circus ramp. I helped Henry turn the Goose around.

"That's it; I'm going home," I declared.

"Thanks for coming partner," Henry smiled. "I'm glad you were along. Enjoy the rest of your day off."

It took me an hour to drive home. I was held up at a railway crossing; two trains. While I was waiting, fog rolled back in.

Chapter Twenty-two

Pipe dreams

Sewer pipes were my first revenue passengers in the Blue Goose. Petterson Construction was installing new sewage lines in Pulpville, a bush town 400 miles north of Circus. The work was nearly finished but the crew was running short of pipe. Petterson called and spoke with Leanne.

"Could someone fly to Gravely Air Park, pick up a load of sewer pipe and deliver it to Pulpville?"

Henry and I were up with students. Leanne checked our bookings and saw a way to make me available.

"Yes," she replied.

"How soon?" Petterson asked.

"I'll call back when the pilot is departing here but it should be around eleven o'clock."

I returned from flying. Leanne gave me her "hurry-up" look when I walked into the office. She spoke up as soon as my student left.

"I juggled things so you could fly a load of sewer pipe to Pulpville for Petterson's," she announced.

"You what?" I gulped.

She frowned. "I booked you to fly sewer pipe to Pulpville in the Goose. They're expecting you at Gravely Air Park around eleven o'clock."

I pictured 12-foot lengths of cast iron pipe, the kind that road crews sling into place with a backhoe.

"We can't carry sewer pipes in the Goose!" I exclaimed. "They're too big and heavy."

"Well, I didn't know. Do you want me to call him back?" she asked.

"No, I will."

"Thank you but before you do," she added quickly, "you should know that he may be a little unhappy with us... I mean, with me."

"Why is that?"

"Well, when he first called, he asked about the invoices I had sent him from last week." She blushed a little. "I told him they were training flights on his airplane for you and Henry." She paused.

I nodded for her to go on.

"He told me that his equipment operators came already trained." Then she dropped into a low voice, mimicking Petterson. "'If they don't come trained, then they don't come,' he declared. 'So why would I pay for pilot training?'"

She paused again.

"And what did you say?"

"I told him that it was his airplane. His construction workers were welcome to fly it for him any time he wanted."

It was easy to picture our take-charge office manager saying something like that.

"What was his reply?" I cringed.

"He didn't say anything at first. He chuckled a little, and then he asked me to send someone for the sewer pipe."

"So we have an unhappy customer who wants us to fly a trip that we can't do?"

"I think so."

I called Petterson. His receptionist answered.

"Hi, I'm calling back from The Flying Circus. I'm afraid your airplane won't carry sewer pipe."

"Hang on," she replied in a husky voice.

Petterson came on the line. "Now what's the problem?" he grumbled.

"Hi, sir. I believe that sewer pipe is too big and heavy to be flown in your airplane."

I took a deep breath waiting for the explosion.

"No it's not," he replied.

"Ah... I think it is... sir."

"OK, you tell me why you think it is and I'll tell you why you're wrong."

"Well... sir..." I stammered, "there is only one small pedestrian door under the wing and the cabin is not very long or wide."

"The cabin is six feet long from the bench seat to the cockpit bulkhead," he sighed impatiently. "We have cut the pipes to fit. I don't see a problem loading them through the door."

"Ah... how much does one piece weigh?" I asked.

"Maybe twenty, thirty pounds."

"Sewer pipe?"

"That's what I'm talking about," he answered gruffly. "What page are you on?"

"I... ah... I thought they'd be heavier."

"They're plastic."

"Oh..."

"Welcome to modern construction. The boys are loading a truck now. It'll be at the Gravely Air Park in 30 minutes."

"I'll be there as soon..."

He had hung up.

"...as I can."

I had a lot to do. I asked Leanne to measure the distance from Circus to Pulpville via Gravely. I still had to move the Goose to the gas pumps, complete a walkaround, calculate how much fuel I needed and determine the weight of sewer pipe I could carry. I also needed to check the weather to the north, see about the facilities at the Pulpville Airport and file flight plans.

I collected the airplane Journey Log and maps in the office and headed outside. I pulled the chocks from the mainwheels on the Goose, jumped in, fired up the engines, taxied ahead to the pumps and shut down. I ran back inside.

Leanne said the route one way was 410 miles. That meant two hours and thirty minutes flying time in no wind. Adding 45 minutes reserve, I'd need 119 US gallons or 713 pounds of fuel. Subtracting 200 pounds for my weight, that left 687 pounds for cargo. I rounded it up to 700 pounds in my head to account for the fuel burned flying to Gravely.

Back outside, I started the gas pump, dragged the fuel hose and ladder to the right wing, climbed up, snapped open the cap, rammed in the nozzle and jammed it on by wedging the fuel cap under the handle. Then I did a quick walkaround and finished fueling.

I was now twenty minutes into my half hour. I decided to check the weather and file flight plans in the air. If the flying conditions were bad up north, I'd land on the way for more fuel. I hopped into the airplane, closed the door, started the engines and called for taxi instructions for a flight to Gravely.

I hurried as much as I dared but was ten minutes late arriving at the air park. An older construction worker stood leaning against the door of a three-quarter-ton pickup truck. He drew slowly on a cigarette while watching me taxi in. Behind him the truck box was piled high with plastic pipe. I powered up the left engine and swung the Goose around so the door side faced the truck.

"Good-day," I said as I hopped out.

The man's work clothes were stretched at their seams. He was big. He looked like he had been in good physical condition years ago but it had slipped. He smiled slightly, which deepened the wrinkles in his pock-marked face.

"Howdy," he replied. His voice was deep and rough. I wondered if everyone at Petterson's construction sounded like aging Texans.

I hustled over to the load. It was six-foot long pipe in three diameters: six-inch, four-inch and two-inch. Each size was a different shade of green. I reached up for a small one on top of the pile and slid it off the back of the truck. It was fairly heavy for plastic; I guessed somewhere

A full load of sewer pipe only reached to the top of the seat cushions.

between five and ten pounds. Petterson's man walked toward me while I pulled out the next two sizes, hefted them and tossed them to the ground. I estimated they were fifteen and thirty pounds each.

"One set of each size weighs about 50 pounds," I declared. "I can take 14 sets."

"Whatever you say captain," the yardman replied. Up close, his face looked like unfinished roadwork. He jerked his thumb toward the truck cab. "I got three, 20-pound boxes of connector rings in the front."

"OK, 13 sets of pipe and the boxes. You take them off the truck and I'll load them into the airplane."

"Roger, roger," he rasped.

He tossed his cigarette away and reached up for a pipe. I picked up the three on the ground. They immediately slid in three directions. I had to drop them beside the fuselage and load one at a time.

My helper seemed to move slowly but he was always ready with another pipe when I had finished working the last one through the door. Five sets covered the floor. I lost some room to the rear-facing seat on the right side but when I had counted to 13 sets, the load only reached to the top of the seat cushions.

"That's it," I called back to my helper.

I turned around. He was standing behind me holding a box.

"Gonna take these?" he coughed.

I loaded three boxes of connectors into the baggage compartment and then looked back at the truck. The remaining pipes were still piled high.

"Can you come back for another load today?" wrinkle-face asked.

I was about to protest but I realized that he was just the messenger. "I'll see how the time goes," I replied. "If I can do another trip today, I'll call your office when I'm refueling at The Flying Circus."

"Sure enough," he nodded.

"It's going to be at least six hours from now," I added.

"You call, I'll be here."

"Before I go, have a look in the cabin so you can see what an airplane load looks like."

He ducked under the wing and looked through the door. "Not much," he wheezed.

"Airplanes aren't like trucks," I explained.

"No, I can see that. What about your other pilot?"

"Why do you ask?"

He pulled a rumpled pack of cigarettes from his shirt pocket and tapped one out. "That pipe you got there," he said, motioning into the cabin, "will keep the boys in Pulpville busy maybe four hours, tops. With a six-hour turnaround, the more you fly, the behinder you'll get. If you stop flying to sleep, we might as well send a truck. Another pilot would help."

The older man was smarter than he looked. "Thanks for the sugges-tion," I said. "I'll hustle out of here and contact the other pilot later."

"OK, partner," he grinned.

"I should see you by six o'clock."

He chuckled a little. "I'll be as ready as an old maid catching flowers at a wedding."

Chapter Twenty-three

Gabby and friends

I scrambled over the dusty load of pipes to the cockpit and discovered the first law of flying freight. If you crawl to the front, you enter the pilot seat headfirst. I pushed myself back, slid around and wiggled in feet first.

I fastened my seat belt, took a deep breath and started the engines. This would be my first departure from Gravely Air Park in the Goose. It was also my first takeoff in the big airplane fully loaded. I tried not to rush but the nature of the flight was go, go, go!

Gravely was a privately-owned airport. The facilities were similar to public airports but minimized to survive without government funding. The single runway was 2,800 feet long and 75 feet wide but only the centre 40 feet was paved. The rest was compacted gravel. In my head I could hear Ziggy saying, "The wheels on the Commander are 18 feet apart. You have an extra 22 feet!"

The night lights along each side of the runway were homemade from inverted peanut butter jars and 25-watt refrigerator bulbs. The little red windsock looked like a leg cut from long underwear.

I turned to wave to my loading helper but his truck was already departing down the gravel driveway. I taxied onto the runway and backtracked to the beginning. I turned the Goose around off the end of the pavement to have the full length of asphalt available.

I stood on the brakes, ran the engines to full power and turned the Goose loose. The airplane obliged. Despite the load, the old girl accelerated rapidly. The big rudder made it easy to stay straight on the narrow pavement. At the 1,500-foot mark, the airspeed indicator reached 80 mph. I eased back on the control wheel, the nose came up and we headed skyward.

I was glad the truck driver wasn't watching. He'd be telling his boss that I short-loaded the airplane to create an extra trip. "Commanders love to fly loaded as long as both engines are running," Ziggy had declared, "but lose one with an overload and you'll be riding a broken elevator straight down."

I climbed the Goose northbound off Runway 04 to 5,500 feet and called the radar controller for Toronto. I crossed Lake Ontario and flew over the east end of the big city. The airline traffic into Toronto International Airport was landing from the other side so I was allowed to continue on course with no conflicts.

I set a heading for North Bay when I was clear of Toronto's air traffic control and called flight service for weather information. The specialist said an area of high pressure covered the route. Conditions were good enough for visual flying all the way to Pulpville. The winds aloft were light and variable. I'd be able to fly non-stop unless something changed.

The Goose was a wonderfully stable airplane to fly. It went where it was pointed, even in turbulence. There was an autopilot on board but I didn't use it. Every 20 minutes, I needed to roll the pitch trim wheel forward one notch as the fuel emptied from the wing to the aft tank behind the cabin. Other than that the big, friendly airplane hummed along holding its altitude and heading.

Ahead the forest was flush with coloured autumn leaves. I sat with my arms folded admiring the scenery while the Goose flew on. I had requested VFR radar following from Toronto Centre but there was little traffic in this low-altitude sector. Further north, the controller told me to switch to North Bay.

"North Bay Terminal, Commander Golf Oscar Oscar Sierra is with you at five thousand, five hundred."

"Golf Oscar Oscar Sierra, radar contact at five thousand, five hundred. I don't have any traffic for you but North Bay GCA requests that you call them."

There was no reason why I should switch to a GCA controller. GCA was "Ground Controlled Approach," a military setup where radar controllers could talk a pilot down in bad weather. I wasn't planning to land at North Bay but I had nothing to lose by calling them.

"I'll switch now," I replied.

"Roger, call me when you're back on this frequency."

"Oscar Sierra."

I changed the radio to the GCA. "North Bay GCA, this is Golf Oscar Oscar Sierra."

"Goosey, Goosey, good day.
This is Gabby, the pilot's friend, on the GCA.
If you have the time,
I have a rhyme."

The cheesy voice sounded like a middle-aged weirdo acting like he was in Grade 4. I didn't know what this was about, but I was curious to find out.

"Go ahead GCA," I replied.

"Hey, hey; my shift ends at three,
In time for tea," the voice giggled,
"But the traffic is down
And if I go to town,
Without one more GCA,
It's a simulator review before another workday.
You'd like to try it I bet,
I'd be in your debt.
If you'd fly a GCA,
In no time you'd be on your way!"

My impression of professional military controllers changed immediately. The stupid part was that I understood the guy. Worse, I caught myself trying to think of a rhyming reply.

"Well, Gabby, I'd like to help," I replied, "but there's a construction crew in Pulpville waiting for this load of sewer pipe to finish a job."

"I don't want to skewer
Your date with a sewer
Tell me, could you help a man,
On your return flight plan?"

"I'm afraid that's a no-go too. I have to do a quick turnaround and go back for another load."

There was a pause.

"So you're on a roundtrip,
Maybe we could fit,
A GCA on your way back,
On the second flight Jack."

"That won't be until nine o'clock tonight," I explained. "You'd have a long shift."

"I get the drift
But not a long shift," he replied in a silly singsong voice.
"I go off to my homes,
Until the terminal phones,
And then I return,
For our date of concern."

I was thinking of declining his invitation so I wouldn't have to listen to any more of his putrid poetry. I had flown practice GCAs before but not in a long time.

"Sure, Gabby," I replied. "It's a date."

"All right,
I'll sit tight!" he whooped.

If Clouds Could Talk

"I'll be nailed to a chair,
Until you're in the air,
On your second return,
Not to be spurned."
"Sounds good."
"Hey, I hope you got,
My thanks a lot."
"I'd better switch back to terminal now."
"You don't have to,
Cause I listen to him too,
And he has no traffic for you."
Gabby was proving hard to ditch so I put him to work.
"Thanks, Gabby. Now can you do me a favour?"
"You name it
And don't you quiver," he answered enthusiastically.
"If I can do it,
I'll deliver."
"Do you have a reference for the Pulpville Airport that tells if it has
fuel and when it's available?"
"A reference here I need not,
The airport guy there is a friend I got.
In cabinets he has 100 octane,
With which he'd be glad to fill your plane.
I'm calling him now,
To assure that no matter how,
He'll be there for you.
It's the least I can do."
"I appreciate it."
A few moments later he was back on the frequency.
"I just talked to my friend,
On him you can depend,
To be there on hand,
As soon as you land."
"OK, Gabby, that's all I need."
He wasn't finished.
"I also arranged for you,
On flight number two,
For my pal to be there,
To get you back in the air.
He also agreed,
That there was no need,
For an overtime charge,
For all my friends at large."

"That's great, thanks again."
"I think I should warn,
My friend's a talker born.
I think in fact,
That he's very bushwhacked."
Bushwhacked, I said to myself, look who's talking.
"Thanks for the tip."
I switched to the terminal frequency before Gabby could spout more fractured verse.

I started a descent toward Pulpville thirty minutes later keeping the power up to gain airspeed and time. Ten minutes out, I selected the airport unicom frequency and transmitted a position report. My call was answered right away. The guy on the mic gave me detailed weather and runway information; advised me of all the traffic that had passed by that day; and told me that the construction crew was there ready to unload my pipe. I was lined up for a landing by the time he finished his first transmission.

I made the mandatory call. "Golf Oscar Oscar Sierra on final for Runway 30 at Pulpville, landing full stop."

The talker immediately launched into advisories about soft shoulders beside the taxiway, the construction truck on the ramp and where I should park. As I turned off the runway, I could see a tall, tow-headed man leaning out of an open window on the one-storey terminal building. He was holding a microphone to his mouth in one hand. He waved at me to park by the fuel pumps while telling me how to do it on the radio.

I followed his directions, set the brakes, shut down the engines and undid my belts. It was two-thirty in the afternoon.

The Petterson Construction pickup truck pulled around the tail of the Goose and stopped on the door side. I could see the talker heading my way. He was bustling across the ramp without actually moving quickly.

I scrambled over the load, opened the door and discovered the second law of freight flying. If you crawl to the door, you have to exit on your hands and knees. Rocky, the foreman, and the Hardy twins stood and watched as I dog-walked from the Goose to the asphalt.

"Hey, it's Stinky," one of the twins said looking down. "Good boy, now sit!"

"Arf," I replied standing up.

Rocky nodded a greeting and pointed the Hardy boys to the load.

The microphone guy puffed his way to our side. "Hi, I'm Montgomery Wordsworth but everyone calls me 'Monty'," he said with an anxious grin. "Gabby told me you were coming. How much fuel do you need?"

"Fill it please, Monty," I replied and pointed to the right wing. "It's single-point refueling on top of the other side."

I turned and saw Rocky holding the door open while Hardy Number One began pulling out pipe and tossing it to Hardy Twin Two who flipped it into the back of the truck.

I looked back at Monty. He was still there, smiling nervously and shuffling his feet.

"One hundred octane?" he asked.

"Yes, that's right."

"OK," he replied. His feet were dancing but they weren't getting anywhere.

I stared at him again.

"Credit card or cash?"

"Card."

"Which one?" he asked hopping from one foot to the other like he needed a washroom.

I pulled out my wallet. "This one!" I replied and handed him a card.

"I'll get right on it," he declared.

He continued trotting on the spot as he turned to Rocky. "He made good time, didn't he?"

Rocky pretended not to hear.

I answered for him. "I'd like to make good time out of here, if I could get some fuel."

Monty gave me a hurt look. "Yes, right away," he answered with mocked respect. He turned and danced toward the pumps, muttering.

I decided that there must be a law in bush flying that says pilots must not be in a hurry and must make small talk with the northern airport operators.

Rocky broke my thoughts. "Olaf said you'll be coming back tonight with another load."

"That's right. I should be here again in six hours."

"Good," the stocky foreman replied. He pointed into the cabin. "This will keep us going today. The load tonight will get us started in the morning. Can you bring one more batch tomorrow?"

"Sure thing," I replied. I had no idea if I could but the look on Rocky's face indicated that "Yes" was the right answer.

"That should be all the pipe we need," Rocky continued. "I really appreciate you doing this." A grateful grin creased his dusty face. "You're saving my bacon on this one," he added.

The Hardy boys were making a quick job of the unloading. I could hear Monty talking to no one in particular from the ladder on the other side. "Prima donna pilots," he muttered loudly, "act like the world revolves around them..."

I followed Rocky's lead and ignored him.

"Why is it your bacon I'm saving?" I asked the foreman.

"We had enough pipe at the start," he replied, "but the locals kept stealing it at night."

"What for? There can't be much market for stolen sewer pipe."

He smiled sheepishly. "Cannons. They were using them for potato cannons."

"Yeah," Hardy Brother One laughed. He continued to pull and toss the pipes. "The kids were having a blast until we built a lock-up for the pipe and the police shut down the propane dealer."

"They should lock those kids up and throw away the key."

"Wow. Was anyone hurt?"

"Naw. Just bruises and singed hair," Rocky replied.

"Yeah, and some busted windows," Hardy One chuckled.

"But you need all three sizes?"

"They started shooting large potatoes with the four-inch pipe" Rocky explained. He was grinning with his head down. "Then they discovered that smaller potatoes in two-inch pipe gave them better range."

"Yeah," the Hardy at the airplane laughed, "and when they ran out of 'taters, they blasted squash out of the six-inchers."

"Someone said they could lob a small pumpkin three blocks," the other Hardy Twin laughed, "but when they tried for further, the pipes blew up."

"Sounds like serious stuff," I mused.

Rocky shook his head back and forth. "They were just having fun."

"Yeah," Hardy One laughed, "now the grocers are rich, the propane guy is out of business and there isn't a barbeque in town that works."

With that, he pulled the last of the pipes from the Goose.

"So we'll see you about nine o'clock tonight?" Rocky said to me.

"Yes sir," I replied.

"OK, thanks again." He followed the Hardy Boys to the truck.

Monty finished fueling. He was still muttering, this time about potato cannons. "They should lock those kids up and throw away the key," he mumbled loudly. "Someone could've been killed."

I listened to his chatter all the way into the terminal building. While he was making out my bill, I telephoned Henry and told him about the multiple trips.

"I'm booked with students this evening," my partner replied. "If you can handle the second trip tonight, I'll do the third one in the morning."

"Sure," I agreed. "That works for me."

"Take your time and be careful," he advised. "We don't get paid if you crash."

"Aye, aye, sir."

I hung up, paid my bill and told Monty that I would be back around nine o'clock.

"I'll be here," he replied. Then he launched into a long explanation about how his overtime worked. I thanked him and walked out. He continued talking.

I fired up the engines on the Goose and turned on the radio. Monty was on the frequency telling me how to activate the lights with my microphone if I returned early and he wasn't there. I couldn't reply or announce my departure while he was transmitting. I took off anyway and flew to Circus.

Henry was on the ground when I arrived. He helped me refuel the Goose and turn it around.

"You'll have to watch your load in the morning," I warned. "One set of pipes weighs about 50 pounds. The Goose can lift 13 sets and three boxes of connectors with enough fuel to go non-stop to Pulpville."

"Thanks. You can tell Petterson that I'll be at Gravely by seven o'clock tomorrow morning."

"Fine. I'll gas the Goose tonight and have it ready for you."

"Don't bother. You'll be tired," Henry replied. "I'll take care of it in the morning."

"I don't mind."

He smiled. "I do. I either fly it after you service it with your bloodshot brain tonight or get up earlier and do it myself."

"You're right. You can get up earlier."

"I will. Have a good trip and take your time."

I phoned Petterson Construction. Olaf answered. I told him that I was on my way to Gravely for the next load.

"The truck will be waiting," he said in his raspy voice.

Then he hung up.

"Good bye," I replied.

Chapter Twenty-four

Backfire

Iflew to Gravely. As I taxied in, I could see the same easy-going yard-man leaning against the truck smoking a cigarette.

"Hi, there," I said stepping out of the Goose.

"Howdy," he nodded.

I walked to the back of the pickup. There were fewer pipes this time.

"That's more like it," I said, pointing to the load.

"It's what the pilot ordered," the older man replied.

Then I realized that all the pipes were the largest size. I reached in and grabbed the end of one to start loading the airplane.

"So they don't need the smaller... what the...?"

I nearly broke my wrist. The pipe was twice the weight of the ones on the last load. I dropped it back into the truck and looked closely. A four-inch and a two-inch pipe were nestled inside the six-inch.

I turned to the workman. "I don't think you understood why I limited the load on the last trip," I explained impatiently. "It's not the size or number of pipes, it's the weight. The airplane can only lift 700 pounds of cargo. Putting the pipes together like this doesn't allow me to carry more."

The man walked over beside me. "You said that one set weighed fifty pounds."

"Correct."

"So you were limited to thirteen sets plus three boxes of connectors."

"Yes."

He pointed to the pipes. "That's thirteen sets." Then he jerked his thumb toward the cab. "The connectors are up front."

"Oh... I get it. I'm still taking thirteen sets but you put them together." My voice sounded more clueless than I knew I could be.

"Correct," he said, mimicking my tone.

"Why put them together?"

"Faster to load and unload."

"Oh... right. Then we better get started."

"I'm ready when you are," he replied with a thin grin.

He picked up one set of pipes as if it was a broomstick and handed it to me. "If it's too heavy, I'll load it for you."

"No, I can manage."

I hefted the pipe; it tipped forward; the other two pipes slid out.

"They don't do that if you keep them level," he said smiling.

"Thanks," I blushed.

Thirteen sets of pipes later, my arms felt longer. I turned to thank my helper. He was standing behind me holding a box of connectors.

"Oh, yeah," I said. "I almost forgot." I loaded the box in the baggage compartment. The workman walked back to the truck for the other two boxes.

When we were done, I asked him to tell his boss that my partner would be back for the last load at seven o'clock in the morning.

"I'll be here," Tex replied.

He climbed into the truck and headed down the road. I crawled into the Goose and took off.

The good weather remained for my second flight north. On the way the sun turned into a rich red globe as it dropped to the horizon, igniting the autumn leaves into a dazzling display of colour. By the time I approached Pulpville, the sun had gone and taken the light with it. The forest below had transformed into a forbidding black carpet.

I heard Monty calling me as soon as I switched the radio to Pulpville Unicom. He clucked away about porcupines on the runway. Then he recited the location and height of all the obstructions within a 100-mile radius.

I landed just before nine o'clock. Rocky and the Hardy boys were waiting on the ramp with the truck. I parked by the fuel pumps, shut down and scrambled out the door, feet first this time. Hardy One was right there. He reached in behind me and grabbed a pipe.

"Hey, somebody finally got smart at the yard and stacked these together," he declared. "We'll be outta here in a minute."

They were. The pipe sets and three boxes were chucked into the truck in no time. They waved their thanks and roared off.

Monty was still on the ladder fueling and talking. "Bears come around here at night," he announced. "They're attracted by human scent. Humans mean garbage and garbage is food."

I half listened to him. It took me a few minutes to realize that I was no longer in a hurry. I had all night to fly home. I sat down on the doorsill of the Goose and relaxed.

"There's no hunting allowed around the airport," Monty continued from above. "Bears know that humans have food; so do the cougars and lynx but there's no food here. There's no telling what they'll do."

"Maybe you could start an airport zoo," I called up to him. "Charge admission."

"I don't think so," he replied without missing a beat. "A bear'd eat a visitor and word would get around. Soon every bear in the province would come here looking to snack on a human."

Monty finished fueling. He talked on about animals as he reeled in the hose and stowed the ladder. He looked over his shoulder often.

I pre-flighted the airplane with a flashlight and then walked to the terminal building to pay my fuel bill.

"Flashlights attract bears," Monty said. "They know humans are the only ones who use them."

"Thanks Monty, I'll keep it in mind. My partner will be back about ten o'clock in the morning with the last load. He'll need fuel then too."

"I'll be here. Now don't forget to backtrack the whole runway to clear the wildlife. Tell your partner about the obstructions. There's one..."

I walked out, took off and headed for North Bay. At 6,500 feet, I leveled off and turned the heater on to ward off the cold. I sat back and let the Goose fly itself. It was a mistake. I fell asleep. I don't know what woke me up. I had turned the radio off to get rid of Monty. Maybe it was the thinner air. The Goose was at ten thousand feet and climbing as the fuel load transferred out of the wing tank. I pushed the trim wheel down and looked around. The lights of a large city appeared under the nose. By the clock, I had been sleeping 30 to 40 minutes.

The lights must be North Bay, I thought to myself.

I turned on the radio and selected North Bay Terminal. The speaker came alive before I could transmit anything.

"Commander Golf Oscar Oscar Sierra, North Bay, do you read?"

The controller paused for a few seconds and then repeated the call. He sounded as if he was trying to wake someone. I didn't know whether to answer him or not. If I did, there would be some explaining to do. I could ignore him and if asked later, say I was overflying the area without calling. Then I remembered Gabby. He was expecting me to do a practice GCA approach at North Bay. Maybe he would call out the air force to intercept me and see what was wrong. Then there would be lots of explaining.

"North Bay, this is Golf Oscar Oscar Sierra. Are you calling me?"

"Affirmative Golf Oscar Oscar Sierra, how do you read this transmission?"

"I read you five. I had my radio turned down and couldn't hear you. Sorry about that."

"Oscar Oscar Sierra, roger. North Bay GCA wants you to call. I have no traffic for you."

"I'll switch now, terminal, thanks."

"North Bay GCA, this is Golf Oscar Oscar Sierra."

"Hey Goosey, Goosey," Gabby's singsong voice boomed through the radio.

"Gabby here,

Have no fear,

While you sleep,

The watch we keep."

"Sorry Gabby, I... ah... had forgotten about our date for a GCA," I lied. "I was cruising along with the radio off."

"It's not too late,

For your date,

With the GCA,

If you say OK."

I was tired and didn't want to practise an approach from 10,000 feet but I felt guilty.

"OK Gabby, let's do it. I need the practice and from this altitude, we'll both get lots of it."

"All right," he cheered,

"Sit tight,

A GCA,

Will come your way."

I had a plan that would keep me awake while having some fun with the pesky poet.

"Commander Golf Oscar Oscar Sierra, this is North Bay GCA."

I couldn't believe that it was the same controller talking. Gabby had dropped his voice an octave and spoke in the neutral tones of a serious controller.

"Turn to a new heading of zero niner zero, vectors for a practice GCA to Runway 26 at North Bay."

"Zero nine zero," I replied.

I was heading south so I turned right, taking the long way around.

"Ah... Oscar Oscar Sierra, that's a left turn to zero niner zero."

By now, the Goose was passing through a heading of west. "Left turn ninety degrees," I replied. I tried to sound like I knew what I was doing. I turned 90 degrees instead of to 090 and rolled out heading south.

"Ah... Oscar Oscar Sierra... what are you doing now?"

"I turned left 90 degrees, like you said. Now I'm going straight."

"OK..." he answered slowly. "Now I'd like you to turn left another 90

Gabby sounded unsure of what to do with this pilot who was flying like a yo-yo.

degrees to a heading of zero niner zero degrees."

"Roger, ninety to ninety," I replied. I cranked the lightly loaded Goose around like a fighter, rolled out of the turn late and corrected back to east. That should have left a squiggly track on his radar screen.

"That's good, Oscar Oscar Sierra. Now for identification purposes, count from one to five and back."

"One two three four five," I transmitted quickly, "five four two three one."

"Ah... close enough, Oscar Oscar Sierra." Gabby sounded unsure of what to do with this pilot who was flying like a yo-yo but he continued.

"You are cleared for a practice GCA approach to Runway 26 at North Bay, Oscar Oscar Sierra. Descend to seven thousand feet and call level."

I read back the clearance. I figured he was positioning me to intercept the glidepath at seven thousand feet. I set up an ultra-slow rate of descent.

"Ah... Oscar Oscar Sierra, can you increase your descent rate?" Gabby asked.

"Affirmative," I replied. I stuffed the nose down on the Goose into a dive. "Approaching seven thousand," I announced almost immediately.

"Ah... Roger Oscar Oscar Sierra. Turn left to a heading of three three zero."

"Three three zero."

"That's correct."

I turned slowly and flew through the runway centreline. I could see the runway lights several miles ahead.

"Oscar Oscar Sierra, further left turn to two four zero."

"Left to two four zero," I replied.

Eventually, Gabby had me near the centreline and the glidepath.

"Oscar Oscar Sierra, you are five miles from touchdown. Configure your aircraft for the final approach and landing. Check your landing gear is down."

"Roger that," I replied nonchalantly.

"Oscar Sierra, do not acknowledge any further transmissions. If you do not hear a transmission from me for any five-second period, initiate a standard overshoot."

I did not acknowledge, as requested.

Gabby waited three seconds and then said, "Oscar Oscar Sierra, you are four point six miles from touchdown on Runway 26 at North Bay. You are slightly right and above the glidepath. Turn left five degrees and increase your descent by 200 feet per minute."

I continued to correct too much or too little, jerking the Goose and Gabby around in the process. It never occurred to me that there were tolerances for the approach.

Near the runway, Gabby pulled me out of the approach. "Oscar Oscar Sierra, you are outside of the approach envelope, initiate an overshoot now," Gabby instructed.

The fun was over but I continued my approach to see what the controller would say next.

He didn't say anything. After five seconds of silence I was obliged to overshoot. I applied full power, started a climb and raised the landing gear. "Oscar Oscar Sierra on the missed approach."

"North Bay GCA checks, Oscar Oscar Sierra is on the standard missed approach," Gabby acknowledged, then his serious tone softened. "You were having some trouble there Goose. How about calling it a night? Land here, stay at my place and depart refreshed in the morning."

I was wide awake. I wondered whether I should confess or not. I didn't want the concerned controller filing a report about a dozy pilot refusing to land.

"My approach was a joke, Gabby," I said lightheartedly. I turned the climbing Goose southbound for home.

"It wasn't that bad," Gabby replied, "but I recommend that you land for the night. How about it?"

"No, really." I scrambled to find the right words. "It was a prank, a joke; I flew erratically on purpose."

There was a pause. "Why would you do that?" Gabby asked slowly and seriously.

"Just for fun, Gabby, honest. You spouted bad poetry so I flew a bad approach. I'm fine to fly home."

"Who said my rhymes were bad?" he replied more seriously.

Now I really didn't know what to say. "How can I convince you that my gyrations on the approach were faked?"

His tone lightened a little. "How about another approach?" he suggested. "If it's a good one, you overshoot and fly home; if it's not, you land and stay over."

"So if I make the approach, I don't land; if I don't make it, I have to land?"

"That's correct."

I didn't want to delay any longer but I didn't want to find out what he might do next.

"OK, you're on. I'm leveling at three thousand feet and turning to a heading of zero niner zero."

"Golf Oscar Oscar Sierra is cleared for a practice GCA approach to Runway 26 at North Bay, maintain three thousand and turn further left to a heading of zero six zero."

Gabby kept up the standard GCA patter but he turned me in much tighter than before. This time he was making me work for it. The Goose was up to the task. She stayed rock solid on every tiny correction I made. We nailed the centreline and the glidepath right on.

"Oscar Oscar Sierra, the runway is one eighth of mile straight ahead of you now, you are on the centre and on the glidepath. This is a practice approach. Initiate an overshoot and then acknowledge this transmission."

I added power and leveled off over the runway, flew along the centreline and then zoomed into a climb.

"Oscar Oscar Sierra is in the overshoot," I transmitted.

"Oscar Oscar Sierra, roger, contact North Bay Terminal. Have a good flight home."

"Hey, thanks Gabby. I'm sorry I messed you up the first time. I thought it would be fun."

"Oh, it was fun all right. My supervisor recorded your radar trace to use in the classroom!"

"There goes the reputation of business aviation," I replied.

"Thanks for doing the second approach. I don't get signed off on a botched one."

"So we're even?"

"Roger that, Goosey." I could hear the smile in his voice.

"On your way back,

Stay safe Jack."

Chapter Twenty-five

Money's worth

"How was your trip?" I asked Henry as he stepped out of the Goose the following morning.

"Interesting," he smiled.

"How so?"

I was ready to hook the tow bar to the nosewheel of the airplane.

"Well, it started out fine," he replied grabbing a propeller blade on the right side to help me to turn the big blue bird around. "You were right about the load. Seven hundred pounds doesn't look like much when it's sewer pipe nestled together but Petterson stuck to your limit."

"Good."

"The flight northbound was OK but I had a strange encounter flying over North Bay."

I guessed what he was going to say next, but I didn't let on.

"Oh?" I said.

"Yeah, I was switched to a GCA controller. The guy was weird. He talked in riddles, called me 'Goosey, Goosey,' and asked if I wanted to practise an approach. I figured he must have mistaken me for someone else."

"Must have."

I turned the tow bar the other way so we could push the airplane back into its parking spot. Henry walked to the other side to push on the left propeller.

"I told him I was going to Pulpville and didn't have time for practice," my partner said.

"Then at Pulpville I met another loony, the airport operator. On the radio and then on the ground he yakked on and on, mostly to himself. He babbled about bears, flashlights, garbage, a zoo, pipes and prima donna

182

pilots. Did you say something to set him off?"

"No, but I think that was the problem. I was in a hurry so I didn't pay much attention to him. That's not the way of the north. You're supposed to arrive at those isolated airports ready to listen."

Henry shook his head back and forth. "Even Rocky was acting funny. He kept thanking me for coming as if I was doing him a big favour."

"I know that story. It has something to do with potato cannons."

"Potato cannons?"

"Yes, that's what the sewer pipes were being used for. I'll tell you all about it later."

"OK. Then, when I was southbound, 'Riddles' the radar guy asked me to land so he could buy me lunch. He sounded like he wanted to take me home."

"Maybe he did. You should have taken him up on it," I laughed.

"No thanks. Bad poets aren't my type."

Later that day, Henry, Leanne and I were having coffee in the office.

"Our corporate calls are dropping off," Leanne announced.

"Yes, I've noticed," Henry replied. "Maybe corporate people don't travel as much toward the end of the year. At least we have Petterson's business."

"True," Leanne said, "but I should have been nicer when he called about the training charges," she confessed.

Henry looked at her in surprise. "What did you say?"

"He complained about being charged for pilot training when he didn't have to train his equipment operators," Leanne explained. "I told him that his drivers were welcome to fly his plane for him any time."

Henry looked at the floor and groaned.

"Do you suppose we'll lose our contract with him?" Leanne asked.

Henry looked up. "What you said won't help."

"I bet he was unhappy when I restricted the loads on those cargo trips," I offered. "It seems whenever I'm involved in one of his calls, I screw up."

"Well, we'd better treat him royally from now on," Henry sighed. "We need his business to keep us going over the winter."

At that moment, the telephone rang. Leanne had just gulped some coffee.

"I'll get it," I said. "Good afternoon, The Flying Circus."

"This is Olaf Petterson," the gruff voice on the other end announced.

"Yes, sir. Mr. Petterson." I gave Henry and Leanne a knowing look. "What can we do for you today, sir?"

"Nothing," he rasped, "but on Thursday I want to fly to the Town of Watt to look at a job."

"Ah... OK..." I stammered. I looked at our wall map but I had no idea where to find Watt. "Ah... where is Watt, Mr. Petterson?"

"West of Thunder Bay. There's a hydro-electric plant going in there and I want to quote on some sewer and water work."

"Ah... our wall map doesn't go that far sir."

"So you can't take me?" Petterson grumbled impatiently.

"No sir... I mean, yes sir, we can take you. I'll just have to dig out another map and call you back."

Henry headed for our map case.

"Well I know where it is," Petterson growled. "It's 700 miles from here which means it's 700 miles back. We can stop in Sault Ste. Marie to refuel. I've arranged to stay overnight in the construction bunks at Watt and return on Friday. Can you do it or not?"

I crossed over to the booking sheets. I had the fewest students. With some juggling, I could do it.

"Yes sir, we can do it."

"I'll see you at the Gravely Air Park at seven on Thursday morning."

"Click." He hung up.

"Fine sir, I'll be there."

Henry had found Watt on the next map. He held it up to the edge of the chart on the wall.

"That's halfway across the continent," I gulped.

"It should be an interesting trip," Henry said, "and a good opportunity to treat Petterson royally."

"It'll be good revenue," Leanne added.

"It's my best chance yet to screw up," I moaned.

I checked the weather on Wednesday. A warm front had rumbled through Watt on Tuesday night followed quickly by a cold front. I called the Watt airport manager to check on the facilities and runway conditions.

"Airport," he answered cheerfully.

"Hi, I'm calling from Circus, near Toronto. I'm planning to fly to Watt tomorrow, landing after lunch. What shape is your runway after the weather you had yesterday?"

"Still long and narrow," he giggled. Then he burst out laughing.

"Have you plowed the snow off yet?" I asked.

"Didn't have to," he answered triumphantly. "It blew off. The runway is clear as glass."

"Great. Do you have 100 octane fuel and parking overnight available?"

"Yes siree," he chirped. "We have lots of fuel and parking on the ramp."

"OK, thanks. I'll call you from Sault Ste. Marie in the morning with

184

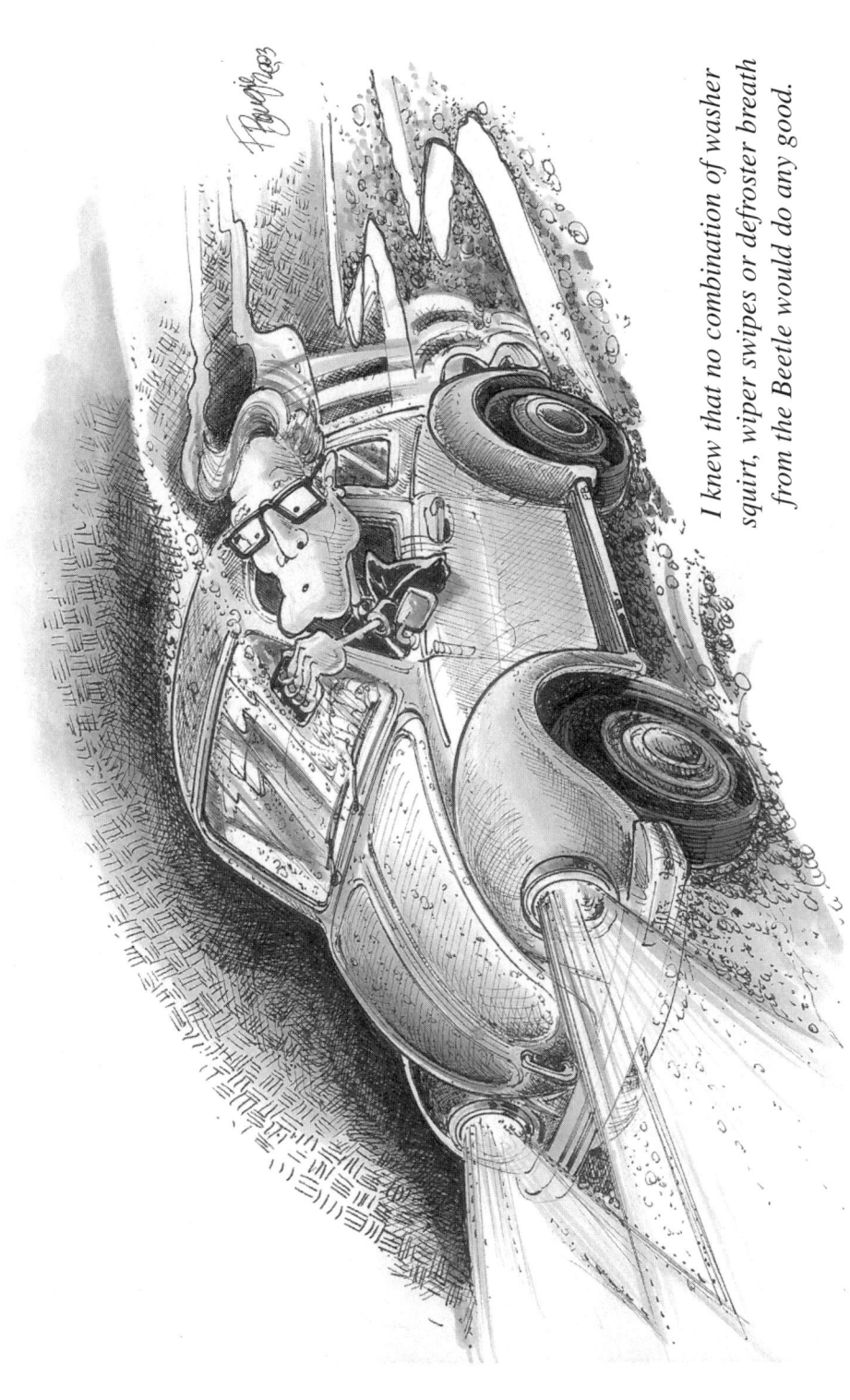

I knew that no combination of washer squirt, wiper swipes or defroster breath from the Beetle would do any good.

our arrival time."

"Rodger dodger," he replied.

I fueled the Goose and checked her over before going home early that evening. I needed to get up at 4:00 a.m. to depart The Flying Circus at 6:30 to pick up Petterson at Gravely by seven. At home I packed a small overnight bag, dressed for the trip and went to bed at 10:00 p.m.

It seemed like I had just put my head down when the alarm went off. I dragged myself out of bed, fed the dog outside, picked up my stuff and fell into the Volkswagen. It was cold and dark.

I crossed my fingers and turned the key. The engine fired, chugged, stumbled and ran. I shifted into first gear and looked ahead. The windows were white with frost. I knew from experience that no combination of washer squirt, wiper swipes or defroster breath that the Beetle could offer would do any good. I rolled down the left side window, stuck my face into the cold air and eased out the clutch. The old Bug jerked its way onto the road. I dug out a twisted credit card from the tray by my knees and reached around with my left hand to scrape frost off the windshield.

I made it all the way to the airport peering through the bottom left corner of the windshield. I didn't hit anything only because at that time of the day, there was nothing on the roads to hit.

The office lights were already on and Henry's Pinto was in the parking lot. I found him unlocking the Goose.

"Good morning," he sang out cheerfully. He sounded like it was normal to meet at the airport at 5:00 a.m.

"It's still dark," I said sleepily. "What are you doing here?"

"Helping you get royally ready and making sure you depart on time," he said.

In the glow of the office lights, I could see why I needed him. The Goose was covered with frost. Even with the two of us it was going to take time to heat the wings from underneath.

"Thank you," I said. The cold was waking me up.

"You're welcome. Throw your stuff into the airplane and then help me rig the heaters."

"Aye, aye, sir."

I unrolled the extension chord to the Goose while Henry placed two car warmers in the cockpit. Then we rolled out the propane heater.

"Run the hoses to the engines," he directed. "Warming the wings takes too long when it's this cold. We'll use rope."

"Rope?"

"You'll see."

I plugged one hot-air hose from the propane heater into the left engine and stuck the other one between my legs under my coat. The blast of hot air warmed me up quickly. Henry came back from the hangar with a 20-foot piece of fat rope. He handed me one end. I pulled the hose out from under my coat and stuck it in the left engine with the other one.

"Stand behind the wing," he said. "We're going to saw the frost off." With that he flipped the rope over the top of the wingtip.

Saw we did. In 30 minutes, we had worked the worst of the frost off all the top surfaces of the airplane.

"I made coffee in the office and Leanne sent muffins," Henry said. "You go file a flight plan and fill the thermos. I'll sweep the rest of the frost off the wings."

"Watch your step up there," I cautioned.

"I know, I know. It'll be slicker than snot on the doorknob."

"That's right," I smiled.

The office smelled like fresh coffee and warm muffins.

It was 6:30 by the time I had checked the weather, filed a flight plan and filled the thermos. I went outside in time to see Henry sliding off the fuselage behind the wing.

"You should be good to go," he declared. "I stored the heaters, extension chord and rope in the baggage compartment."

"Thanks a million."

"You're welcome."

I was wide awake by the time I had the Goose on the runway ready to go. I pushed the throttles all the way to the stops, released the brakes and held just a light back pressure on the control wheel. I let the Goose tell me when she was ready to go in case some residue frost reduced the lift. There was no delay. The old girl rotated at 80 mph and took to the air.

Eight minutes later I was circling the dark spot on the ground where I knew the Gravely Air Park was. I clicked my microphone button five times on the unicom frequency to activate the peanut butter jar lights. The two rows of tiny bulbs winked on below. There was no wind so I joined the circuit to land toward the turnoff near the south end. The path between the lights looked narrow. It was narrow. Approaching in a twin-engine airplane at 90 mph made it appear skinnier than ever.

On final, the mistake I needed to avoid was descending through the runway while waiting for it to grow to a normal width. I consciously forced myself to look part way down the strip. I watched for the lights to come up to my level. They did, quickly. I flared out a bit late. The mainwheels squealed in protest as they hammered onto the runway. I squeezed the brakes. They were working but I was going too fast. I braked harder. The nose came down. I sailed past the turnoff. The Goose stopped just before the end. I turned her around and taxied in.

A light above the hangar outlined the figure of a man. I shut down and stepped out. The man moved forward. He was wearing a hardhat and carrying a battered briefcase. He was chuckling.

"I see you got your money's worth from the runway that time," he said.

I recognized the rough voice of my loader friend from the Petterson Construction yard.

"Hey Tex, what are you doing here?"

"You and I are going to Watt," he replied.

"Where's your boss?"

As soon as I said it, I realized that I must be talking to Petterson himself. My jaw dropped. You could have stuffed two feet in my gaping mouth.

"You're Petterson?"

"Olaf Petterson," he replied.

"Ah... sir... I'm sorry. I didn't know who you were yesterday..."

"No problem," he answered calmly. "I should have introduced myself but you were busy being in a hurry."

"I was in a hurry."

"I know, one load in a pickup truck equals three loads in the Commander."

"I was trying to do the job right," I said defensively.

"That's fine with me," he replied. The voice was gravely but the tone was friendly. "And you got the job done. I appreciate it."

I realized he was being complimentary.

"Are we ready to go?" he asked.

"Yes sir, climb in," I said motioning to the cabin.

Petterson ducked through the doorway and settled on the bench seat in the back. I showed him how to work the seat belts and the door latch.

"Don't worry," he grinned, "I hate flying but I won't jump out."

"Good," I smiled back nervously. I could feel my face was still red from discovering my loader friend owned the airplane and the company. "The coffee and muffins are here," I continued. "Help yourself any time."

"Not now, but thanks."

"Over here is a blanket and a pillow."

"I'll be fine," he replied.

His voice was telling me to cut the royal treatment and get under way.

"You take care of the flying," he said, "and I'll worry about the passenger."

"Yes sir."

I went forward and slid into the pilot seat. I got busy starting the airplane and taxiing out. I quickly forgot my embarrassment.

The wind was still calm, so I lined up on the runway facing northbound. To the right, the first light of the November dawn was washing the darkness out of the eastern sky.

I turned to look at my passenger. He was slouched in his seat with his eyes closed. I applied full power. The Goose leaped forward, her props finding good thrust in the cool air.

I climbed to 4,500 feet, leveled off and set a course to Sault Ste. Marie. One hour and forty-five minutes later, I reduced the power to descend to the airport.

I felt a tap on my right shoulder. Petterson had moved forward to the seat behind the cockpit partition. He leaned into the front.

"Are we in the Sault already?" he asked. He was peeling the paper off a muffin.

"Yes, sir," I replied, "but don't open the door until after we land."

He smiled and gave a short, guttural laugh.

We landed and taxied to the fuel dealer's ramp. Petterson went to the washroom in the little office while I checked the airplane over during the refueling.

Petterson walked back out. "Is there a restaurant in the terminal?" he asked pointing to the next building.

"Yes, sir," I replied.

"Those muffins were good but I could use some breakfast. Do we have time for that?"

"Yes, sir. This is your airplane and your trip. We do whatever you want, when you want."

"Hey, hey," he grinned. "I like it."

We walked over to the terminal. Petterson ordered the lumberjack special. So did I.

While we waited, the construction boss grinned and said, "That's quite a powerhouse receptionist you have in your office."

I blushed, remembering Leanne's comment when he had complained about the training charges.

"Leanne is more than a receptionist. She runs our office," I replied. "I heard she was a little short with you over the training invoice."

He chuckled. "In my business, I appreciate a direct answer and she gave it to me."

"Sorry about that."

"No problem. I just don't like surprises. As long as I know what's coming, I'm fine."

"I'll tell her."

"What's important to me are results," he continued in a fatherly tone, "but I don't cut corners. As long as I'm getting my money's worth, I'm glad to pay." Then he grinned. "Your girl and I will get along fine but I wouldn't want to be married to her. She too honest."

"She's Henry's wife," I said.

Petterson winced and then giggled. "So she runs him too?"

"They make it work."

He nodded knowingly.

Our breakfasts came. During the meal, I asked Petterson why he purchased an airplane when he didn't like flying.

"I don't like flying or driving," he replied, "but flying is quicker. This trip has been good so far. I slept most of the way."

"Henry said you don't like going high."

He tapped his chest. "I have a little heart condition. I pass out from a lack of oxygen on airline flights."

"Well, the sun is up and the scenery around the north shore of Lake Superior is spectacular," I said.

"You're the pilot. Just get us to Watt."

Petterson called his office while I telephoned the weatherman and then the Watt Airport before we departed on the final leg. The weather was to remain cold but clear. I gave the airport manager my estimated time of arrival and asked him again about the runway conditions. He assured me that the runway was open. "There's not a scrap of snow on it," he declared.

At my invitation, Petterson sat up front in the right seat. We took off and headed northwest. I leveled off at 1,000 feet, just above the tops of the craggy hills that ringed Lake Superior. I guided the Goose through gentle turns to stay over the irregular pattern of inlets. Alternating arms of rock and water rolled underneath the airplane's nose. We were in the front row seats of a giant, live theatre. Occasionally a road snaked close to the shore, connecting the isolated settlements to the outside world.

"This is a great way to see the country!" Petterson declared.

We exchanged stories about ourselves and our careers while marveling at the rugged, unspoiled terrain sliding beneath us. Petterson told me that the airplane was part of a plan to expand his business. This trip was the first step.

Later, the big contractor retreated to the bench seat in the cabin for another snooze.

I was feeling good. I was learning what made Petterson tick. We were cementing a good customer/supplier relationship. I decided that The Flying Circus would be able to keep Petterson's business, baring any other problems.

I was also pleased with the direction Henry and I had taken. The corporate flying had generated more business. It was also expanding our personal horizons as pilots and people. If we could keep it going, I could see more airplane management contracts like Petterson's. Maybe we would hire more instructors for the flying school. Things were looking up.

The Goose cruised along without missing a beat. The powerful, deep-throated hum of its engines was reassuring as we left the lakeshore and headed west over dense forest. I climbed higher and navigated by the patchwork of lakes and streams that dotted the bush.

Petterson woke up when we were less than an hour out of Watt. He moved to the seat behind the cockpit and leaned forward.

"Where are we?" he asked.

I held up the map and showed him. "Right here," I replied. "We just crossed into the next time zone. It's an hour earlier here. We'll be landing in 50 minutes."

"Do we still have coffee and muffins?"

"Yes," I replied, "they'll be cold but help yourself."

"Do you want any?" he asked.

"Sure, if there's enough."

Petterson poured coffee into two of the plastic cups that Leanne had provided and handed one to me. "Here you go," he said.

"You're hired," I replied.

He grunted his little laugh and sat back in his seat. "Now I feel like I'm working," he declared. "Cold coffee and hard muffins, just like on a construction job."

"Cheers," I said, holding up my cup.

"Cheers."

I radioed to Watt on the unicom frequency when we were 20 minutes out. The enthusiastic voice of the airport manager answered right away.

"Golf Oscar Oscar Sierra, this is Watt Unicom, go ahead."

"Watt, Oscar Sierra is twenty minutes to the east at four thousand, landing Watt, request airport advisory."

"Oscar Oscar Sierra, Watt, the wind is from the northwest at ten to fifteen knots, slightly favouring Runway 22. We have no reported traffic."

"Roger Watt, Oscar Sierra will call overhead the airport joining a right downwind for Runway 22. Would you please call us a taxi. We have two people going to the new hydro site."

"Affirmative, Oscar Oscar Sierra, will do."

Petterson moved into the right front seat.

"I decided that the safest place is beside the pilot," he said with a grin. "If you stay alive, so do I."

"You're right," I replied.

I called in a position report and looked down at the airport as we turned overhead. The runway appeared clear. The windsock indicated a 90-degree crosswind from the right on Runway 22.

"Oscar Oscar Sierra," the manager said cheerfully, "the wind is three

If Clouds Could Talk

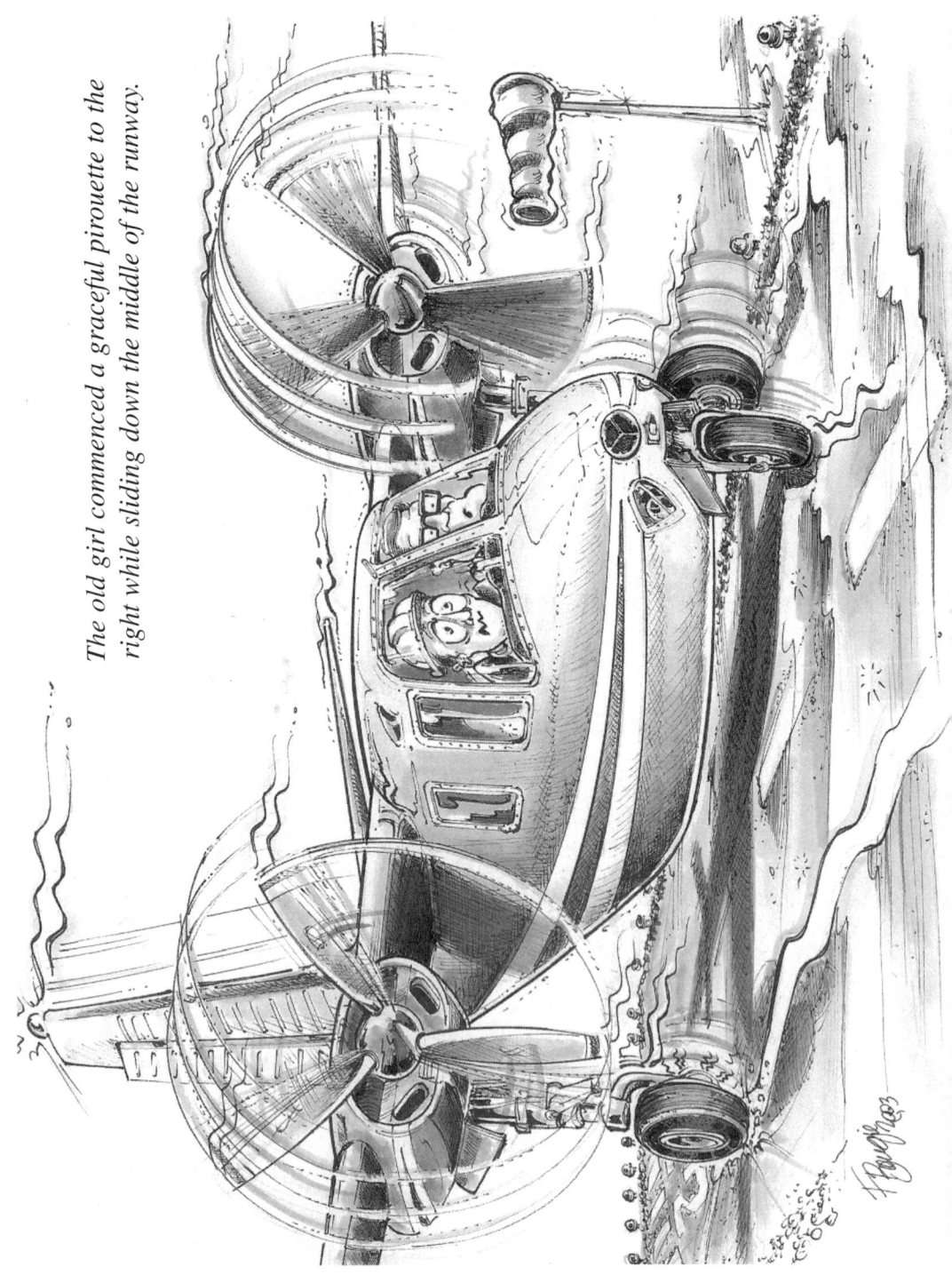

The old girl commenced a graceful pirouette to the right while sliding down the middle of the runway.

zero zero at ten to fifteen. There is no reported traffic. Your taxi cab is on the way."

"Oscar Sierra, thank you."

I turned the Goose parallel to the runway on a right downwind leg, slowed down and completed a pre-landing check.

"Seat belt tight?" I asked Petterson.

"I'm in," he replied. He looked a little apprehensive.

"We are doing a right-hand approach," I explained. "Next I'll start a descent and turn right again to line up with the runway. We'll be landing that way," I pointed toward Runway 22.

He smiled a little nervously. "You're the pilot. Just get us down safely."

I smiled back, "OK boss."

I carried an extra five miles per hour on the final approach to make it easier to correct for the crosswind. I flared out over the threshold holding the right wing down slightly with the aileron. The Goose hung over the runway for a moment. I pulled the throttles all the way to idle. The straight pipes on the exhausts echoed with a few pops and rumbles. The right wheel touched. I pinned it there by feeding in more aileron. Then the left wing came down and the left wheel contacted the runway. There was no squeal or chirp from the tires. I squeezed both brakes and relaxed some back pressure on the control wheel. The nose dropped but the airplane was not slowing down enough. I checked the left wheel out my side window. It was not turning.

The runway was covered in a solid layer of clear ice. I decided we had passed the point for a safe go around. I pulled the control wheel all the way back and pumped the brakes. The temperature must have been perfect for ice skating but not for stopping. The three-ton airplane continued down the runway at speed. The crosswind was urging it to swing to the right. I started to correct with opposite rudder and then changed my mind. The far end of the runway was coming up quickly. I booted the right rudder, pumped the right brake and added power to the left engine. The Goose obeyed. The old girl commenced a graceful pirouette to the right while sliding down the middle of the runway. We swung through the 90-degree point. I shoved the right throttle lever up and pushed the left rudder pedal all the way in. The rotation slowed but continued through the centreline. I applied more power on the right side. Then I matched it on the left. We were now sliding blindly backward. I went to full power on both engines. The blast from the propellers gave me some rudder control. I was able to keep us straight as we skated tail first at decreasing speed. I had no idea how much runway was remaining. I held on and waited for the crunch that would come when we dropped into the ravine off the end.

It never came. The Goose stopped sliding and started creeping forward. I reduced the power. My chest hurt. I was holding my breath. I let it out and taxied very slowly toward the turn-off mid-way down the runway. I had to carry extra power on the left engine to keep the crosswind from weathercocking the Goose to the left. The result was a half-crab and half-slide down the middle.

I finally chanced a look at my passenger. Petterson's eyes were wide, his hands were clamped onto the arms of his seat and his shoulders were hunched up around his ears.

"What happened?" he asked in a tight voice.

"That was a very exciting but happy landing," I replied, jockeying the throttles to track straight. "Mister Airport Manager neglected to mention the layer of clear ice in his runway report."

"I didn't know airplanes could turn around and stop like that," Petterson squeaked. He was still holding on as if the ordeal was not over.

"Either did I until two weeks ago," I replied. "You can thank the training that you paid for, for that."

My comment launched him into a nervous giggle. I looked his way again. His shoulders were shaking with contained laughter. The giggles grew louder.

"I haven't paid that bill!" he declared with a huge grin.

I started to laugh too. It wasn't a good joke but it cut through our tension.

"Maybe we should go back up and try that landing again," I teased.

"Oh, no! I'll pay, I'll pay!" he sputtered. "I got my money's worth and more!"

About the Author

Garth Wallace is from St. Catharines, Ontario, near Niagara Falls, where he learned to fly in a Fleet Canuck in 1966. From 1971 until 1990, Garth worked full time at various locations as a flying instructor, bush pilot and corporate pilot. It was during those flying years that he met the colourful characters and lived the humorous experiences that are the basis for his six-book series of funny flying stories. Garth now lives near Ottawa, Ontario, Canada with his wife Liz.

About the Artist

Francois Bougie's interest in aviation was sparked at an early age by his father who restored several aircraft and constructed two homebuilts. Francois' passion led to a college education as an aircraft maintenance engineer and a career as an electromechanical designer in the aerospace industry in Montreal, Quebec. In the 1990s, Francois began applying an artistic talent to aviation art and industrial technical illustrations. His work has been published on several aviation book covers, posters and in aviation magazines. Francois is a licenced pilot. He has owned a Cessna 120 and a Pitts Special. He currently flies a classic 1946 Globe Swift that he restored.

Other books by Garth Wallace

If Clouds Could Talk is the sixth book in a series of funny flying stories written by Garth Wallace. The next four pages contain information on the previous five funny tales plus other books on aviation and humour published by Happy Landings.

Fly Yellow Side Up

Fly Yellow Side Up is the hilarious story of a suburban pilot who moves north seeking the freedom and glory of flying floatplanes. Follow Wallace as he takes a bush pilot job with no floatplane experience and stumbles his way into the fascinating world of wilderness flying.

Soft cover

Pie In The Sky

Laugh with Wallace as he learns that the riches to be found running a small town flying school are in the characters and the memories. In *Pie In The Sky* Wallace discovers cowboy agricultural pilots, Mennonite buggy buzzing and other off-the-wall aviation adventures.

Soft cover

Derry Air

Flying students Marathon Melville and Beautiful Bob, aircraft owner Barnacle Bill, linecrew Huey, Duey and Louey, Manager Stingy Mingy and the wonderfully sarcastic ground school instructor "Dutch" are some of the crazy characters in *Derry Air.*

Soft cover

Cockpit Follies

This book is the sequel to *Derry Air* in Garth Wallace's series of funny flying stories. Bull Muldoone, Marathon Melville and Skid Sicamore are joined by a new cast of crazy characters. Soft cover

The Flying Circus

Get ready to laugh again as Happy Landings presents more funny flying stories by Garth Wallace. *The Flying Circus* is the humourous tale of two instructors who start a flying school with loads of enthusiasm, little business sense and no money.

Soft cover

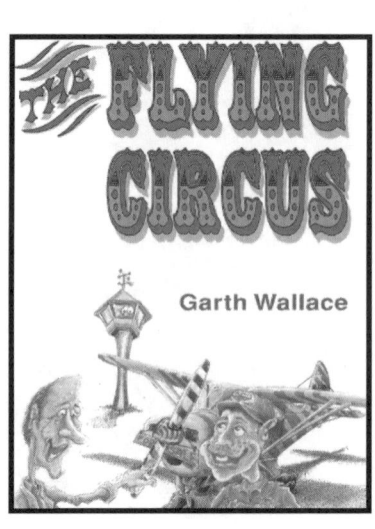

An aviation biography by Garth Wallace

Don't Call Me a Legend

Don't Call Me a Legend is a true adventure story about a modern-day aviation legend. This inspiring biography follows Charlie Vaughn as he works his way from sky-gazing farm boy to a world renowned ferry pilot. Fly with Charlie as he delivers a Cessna Skymaster to Botswana, a Twin Otter across the Pacific, a Hawker Siddeley through Russia and many other global adventures.　　　　Hard cover

Other books published by Happy Landings

Papa X-Ray - by Jim Lang

Papa X-Ray is the true story of a trusty old airplane, a family adjusting to life in the far north and a greenhorn pilot learning to fly in the spectacular ruggedness of Canada's Northwest Territories. Follow Jim Lang as he trades a trailer for an airplane and flies it as family transportation through the wilderness around Nahanni Butte.　　　　Soft cover

Ace McCool - Jack Desmarais

Ace McCool spoofs the airline industry through the laughter-packed exploits of Down East International, a fictional "fly-by-night" operation based in Moncton, New Brunswick. These tall tales brought laughter to thousands of aviators reading *Canadian Aviation* magazine. Now, for the first time, they have been assembled in a collector edition book. Soft cover

Magnetic North - by David Halsey

Magnetic North chronicles a coast-to-coast trek across northern Canada by foot, dogsled and canoe. What started as the Trans-Canada Expedition became a gripping adventure for two young men who set out to rediscover the Canadian North the hard way.   Hard cover

---

Happy Landings books are available at pilot shops, aviation museums, book stores or via direct mail order from the publisher.

Ordering books published by Happy Landings

Happy Landings accepts phone and fax orders with VISA or MasterCard, and mail orders with cheque, VISA or M/C

**Telephone: 613-269-2552
Fax: 613-269-3962
Mail: Happy Landings
RR # 4, Merrickville
Ontario Canada K0G 1N0
Internet: www.happylandings.com
E-mail: books@happylandings.com**

Please mention if you would like your books by
Garth Wallace autographed by the author